MAKE MONEY IN MUSIC
without being a star

blackchili

Dedicated to Peter, Dorothy, Leslie and Grace, to whom I owe so much

A catalogue record for this book is available from the British Library.
ISBN: 978-1-911064-03-9

Published by Black Chili Limited
For more information, please email publications@blackchili.co.uk
Cover design by mmimusicbooks.com

CONTENTS

Foreword

The majority of books you read about 'making it in the music business' will try to sell you a formulaic approach to becoming a bubble-gum pop star. They will explain the prevalent myths that they believe are preventing everyone from being the next big thing. They will offer you 'secrets', things 'the pros' do to succeed beyond us mortals. They will claim to teach you how to reinvent yourself, correct past mistakes and become a star.

But their approach is wrong.

Some of the advice offered is well-meaning, and much of it has an element of truth to it. But if the approaches offered in other books really worked, would their authors not already be stars, and would the world not already be full to bursting with readers of 'be a big star' books who fill the music charts today with their amazing work? What's that? You have never heard any of the big names in the business thank the authors of such books for unleashing their potential and unlocking the secret door to fame and wealth? Well, that's weird isn't it...

The facts of the matter are that the chances of hitting it big in the music business are infinitesimally small - around the same as the chances of being a big Hollywood star. Around 1 in 1,500,000. If playing the odds, you'd be just as wise to buy ten lottery tickets and wait for your jackpot. The lottery is actually a better bet since you could have another go next week. Framed in those terms, hopefully it is as apparent to you as it is to me that you might be waiting a while for fame. But do not despair!

Fundamentally, success is in your own hands. If you have the will to succeed, build a solid plan and have the determination to follow it through in spite of all the challenges you will inevitably face, you will succeed sooner or later. The problem is that success is unlikely to arrive overnight, where your need for food and a roof over your head is pretty urgent. This is the reason for society's two primary impressions of the musician: the huge star and the starving artist. You either make it or fail utterly. This is also the reason that anyone with any sense will tell you not to covet a career in music because your chances of being a big star are slim, and the alternative is catastrophic. And if that was true they'd be doing you a favour dragging you out of the fire. But they're wrong.

There is hope!

It is true that there are a relatively small number of wildly successful musicians in the world. It is also true that there are a huge number of musicians who now work in supermarkets, shops, cafes and all manner of other bill-paying vehicles of soul destruction. Their means to an end. But that is not inevitable. What the books on music superstardom and the societal view of all-or-nothing careers in music overlook is the simple truth that the vast majority of musicians are perfectly successful. Every professional musician out there is successful on their own terms; they survive on the income they generate with their passion for music. So, if you're looking to be successful in the music business, think about what success looks like to you. There is one 'secret' that all the books and Internet articles fail to share, and it is the most fundamental one out there:

You do not need to be a star to make money in music.

Yes, you heard right, but here it comes again. Louder, just to make sure: YOU DO NOT NEED TO BE A STAR TO MAKE MONEY IN MUSIC! Stories of the majority of working musicians do not register with the wider world, because they lack the excitement of the guys you see on MTV. But they are out there - a silent majority of musicians and music professionals who make very good incomes from music, in spite of all the warnings they heard just like you did. Their prospects are just as good as those of any other profession. Their livelihoods no less secure. It could, in fact, be argued that they're more secure since a self-employed musician is unlikely to fire themselves when times are tough. They are out there working and living their dream. They have turned their passion into their day-job. And you can too.

When embarking on a career in music, it is a good idea to examine your motives. It is unlikely you want to be a star anyway; you want the trappings of stardom. You want to be wealthy and think of fame as a means to achieve that wealth. But why do we want to be wealthy? Probably to distance ourselves from all the concerns a lack of money can bring. To give ourselves freedom. But why do we want freedom? To unburden ourselves from obligation and give ourselves the gift of time to spend with family and friends, and to do as we please. So, you didn't want to be a star anyway; you wanted to be successful enough that you could stop having to do stuff you didn't want to do. Well good news: we can do that here for sure!

No Secrets

It is traditional in a book such as this to make the reader wade through to the end to unlock the secrets within. There are no secrets here. This book is split into sections based on the facets of the music industry in which the author has very successfully made an income, and the author is not a star - which explains the title. This book offers many incremental answers that can be combined based on your interests, available time, current skills and experience, and tolerance for failure. You will be encouraged to be a jack of all trades and ideally the master of a couple, though that is not compulsory. To always be prepared for, and say yes to, an opportunity... and then figure out how you're going to do it.

And you can do it, just as the author has done it using the methods that follow.

Introduction

From the moment I saw Eric Clapton play guitar at age 8, I wanted to be a rock star. Probably just like every other kid who ever picked up a guitar wanted to be a rock star. It was a rocky road - armed with a cheap plywood classical guitar and a teacher who taught some very dull group lessons where 'Mull of Kintyre' was about as rock and roll as it got, I had a mountain to climb. Over my adolescence, I became a passable cellist and a pretty technically accomplished guitarist - true to my roots I remained a genuinely awful pianist. I still am, you can't be good at everything.

On to higher education, and I had bought the line that so many other people hear - that a career in music is not really an option, it is not really a career. It is certainly not a sensible thing to aspire to, and the chances of achieving it are somewhere in the slim to nil range. I wonder if you've heard the following joke, which sums up that whole thought ballpark:

> *"What is the difference between a large
> pizza and a musician?...*
>
> *...A pizza can feed a family of four."*

Haha! And thus, with my dreams appropriately filed as dreams, my hobby remained my hobby. I completed my studies and embarked on a very lucrative career in technology. I always played guitar - all the way through University I played in bands, taught a few lessons and busked at train stations until I had enough money for the fare. Whilst working I continued playing in bands and with friends. We never hit it big but became moderately well known within our genre, did successfully complete a national tour, and had a modest local following.

I've always had ambition. When I was earning £11K at my first job, I wanted to know how I could earn £22K. Having gotten the skills and qualifications that were the gatekeeper for that level of job, I found out how to earn £44K. I made a plan and set about checking all the boxes. Pretty soon I achieved that and straight away wanted to find out about £88K jobs. I was earning very good money. I was also, sadly, working extremely long hours under intense pressure. I got all the way to 25 before I started getting chest pains, and maybe most of the way to 26 before I started to lose track of myself.

It was around about that time that work got really stressful, I was really rundown, and an opportunity arose to take a second look at the path I was following. The moment that triggered it all was not tremendously positive; I had what people would probably think of as a bit of a breakdown. The positive outcome was that I managed to look at myself from outside, and see extremely clearly what I needed to do. Take stock, figure out a goal and make a plan. Just like I'd done to build the career I had, but with a better one in mind. Matching my salary to the penny from working in music would have been too great a challenge for overnight, so part of my process had to be about my definition of success. Though I was earning a lot of money, I didn't *need* a lot of money. I could have lived off less than half of my salary, I figured I needed around £30K per year to pay all my bills and have enough money for a few luxuries alongside the necessities. My car would need to last longer, and maybe I'd need a part-time job to pay for a holiday. Maybe if I enjoyed my life enough, I wouldn't feel like I *needed* a holiday at all! But if I could earn £30K per year from music, I could live a happy life. I consider that being successful.

Despite my predilection for dreaming, I have always been an intensely practical person. My Dad was a bank manager, and try I as I might whatever subliminal impact there was from that left its mark. I had a house, bills, and dependants. There was no way I could simply quit my job, pick up my guitar and head into the big wide world with nothing but my dreams and determination (and my guitars of course). So pretty quickly I figured out that an almighty thunderbolt of luck was reasonably unlikely, and therefore stardom, were it to come at all, would not come quickly. I did not have the time to wait for my luck to come in, or for my magic moment to arrive. I had to eat in the meantime if nothing else. I had already had a taste of living the rock and roll lifestyle: touring, sleeping half the day, being up all night. Probably drinking too much. Probably doing most things too much. Never being at home and rarely seeing family and friends. And I didn't want that. I wanted to make a living from music because I love music, but as it turns out I didn't actually want to make it big!

I think it too big of a risk to pursue music the rock star way. Boom and bust. Even those who make it usually do not last for long. The world is a famously fickle place, and a record deal, whilst made by one record, can be destroyed by the next. I knew I needed to adopt several strategies and avenues for success to assure an income.

There are several advantages to the 'jack of all trades' approach, though it is admittedly helpful to master a couple. If you turn your hand to several things you can shift priorities as your interests come and go; you can cover any drop in income from one sector with an increasing attention to another, and often the skills and experience acquired are complimentary. If you become a better tutor; you'll be a better player. If you become a better composer; you'll write better songs. If you write more music you'll get more exposure, which will lead to more work. One giant upward vortex!

I started my journey into music with the advantage that music had always bubbled in the background. Even whilst working my day job I had been teaching, playing, recording and participating on the Internet (forums and fan sites primarily) so there was the opportunity to build an extra income. And that became the plan. In the short term, it meant I was even busier than before as I worked a 9 to 5 as well as forwarding my music interests on evenings and weekends, but the passion I had to succeed removed any pain from that process. I didn't sleep much for a few months, but it didn't take long for it to start being worthwhile.

So I started opening my eyes to opportunity. And as soon as I did opportunity was everywhere. I started moderating an Internet forum with over a million users as a volunteer. Before long I was being paid, then I was being paid more to write articles for a newsletter, lessons, and transcripts of recordings. And then a bit more to edit the contributions of others. Then I was getting free gear to review for the newsletter that I could give away in competitions. My music teacher was also an in-demand session player who couldn't fulfil all the engagements he was invited to participate in, so he recommended me. Previous gigs in my local area meant the owners of venues knew me. Have an act cancel? Give me a call. Maybe a band's guitar player fell over and broke his hand? Give me a call. I recorded EVERYTHING, becoming an engineer and producer. I still record everything. And in amongst the filler there will be an occasional bit of killer. I collate that and turn it into a saleable product.

The list above is neither detailed nor exhaustive but gives an insight into one of the main keys to being a success in the music industry. Versatility. I have always had the drive to do things myself. I get frustrated when I can't do something, so I go and figure out how. By wanting to do everything, and by becoming capable in many areas of the business, I am able to make myself useful in lots of different ways to all kinds of people. And in music just like any other trade, when you are useful, people will want to employ you. If you become really useful you may find you have more work than time in which to do it. And when you get there, your prices can go up. I love variety. I'm told it is the spice of life - it certainly stops me going crazy. The more work you do, the more people you meet. The more people you meet the more opportunities come your way. Do your job well and treat people well, and you will always have more work than you need. And suddenly you've become successful in the music business, you've made money and you didn't need to become a star to achieve it.

And as we speak of ever-increasing opportunity - never say no. Or at least don't say no until you've given it a good go. You may not see it now, but not being a star has some really big benefits. Until I played classical guitar at a wedding, I had never played classical guitar at a wedding. I was a bit out of practice and hadn't played classical guitar at all in several years. I was very nervous of being a let-down, but I also really needed the money. I considered the worst-case scenario, which I judged to be not playing as well as I hoped I would. I knew I would play well enough for the audience, and I wouldn't want to let down a customer, nor ruin a special day. So I took the job, and it went really well. It isn't really my 'thing', so I don't seek work playing at functions, but if somebody asks I wouldn't say no. If I was famous, the risks associated with making a fool of myself would be greater, the risks of failure would be greater, and the impact on future work of that failure is also likely to be more significant. Little old me, who nobody has ever heard of? The blast radius on that one is going to be a good deal smaller, and likely a lot more survivable. So, grasp opportunity with both hands, particularly if opportunity means money. We want to make a living here, and there is no shame in being a jack of all while you work at mastering a few.

The Internet has completely revolutionised the music business, the routes to market we all have available to us and the tools we can use to get there. You can teach yourself just about anything if you have the patience to do so. And I recommend you do. Doing everything yourself gives you absolute control, minimises your costs and makes you more valuable as a musician. If a producer has the choice of a session guy, or a session guy who can read music and has a background in composition, who do you suppose he will get the better result from? If you get to the point where there are things it is more economically viable for you to pay somebody else to do, by all means do so. Even then, if you ask someone to do work for you that you could do yourself, you can give their work proper quality control and be confident in the results.

We all know music's megastars, with their huge houses, fast cars, and fat bank balances. We've already been reacquainted with the archetypal musician who is less useful than a large pizza. This book will detail several areas of the music business that allow the enormous number of musicians who live very comfortably between these two extremes to do so happily, and with as much stability and security as is possible in today's world. Over the last 5 years I have, on average, made in excess of £85K every year from music. I got my last mortgage approved on solely the income from music. My interests have become many and various over the years, so I will not claim 100 percent of my income is derived from music now, but it has been in the past, and I could easily live on my music income today.

I have made plenty of mistakes over the years. Plenty! But if you get your mind right you can consider each an opportunity, even if it is only the opportunity not to do the same thing next time. I found my own path in music, becoming self-sufficient before I could truly consider myself 'successful'. I had the advantage of a childhood spent learning multiple musical instruments, but the disadvantage of being talked out of music as a career. I had the advantage of a day job that would cover my necessities while I built a solid alternative, but the disadvantage of it taking an enormous amount of energy which I would have much rather used for music. You might be a better musician than me, you will almost certainly be a better business person than me, and if you're not a better pianist than me... don't do that for a living. Seriously. You cannot fail to be a better musician than half the people you see on MTV, so make the most of the combination of talents you hold that is unique to you, and go for it!

I had only been playing around 3 years when I started being paid for it - you absolutely DO NOT need to be the best player of your instrument in the world. You need to make the most of what you have and play to your strengths. I am, for instance, a pretty inventive lead guitar player, but I'm a distinctly average rhythm player. I don't enjoy it particularly, it is not where my interests lie – though I continue to work on it in the spirit of bettering myself as an artist. What do I do with that? Play to my strengths. When I play rhythm I 'cheat' by adding a lot of fills and lead lines to keep myself interested. If I'm given a score to play, no problem - my personal challenge is imagination with chords rather than the mechanics of playing. But I overcome. Making a living as a musician is no less challenging than any other career based on talent, but it is very achievable if you're dedicated and passionate enough to overcome the inevitable setbacks you will encounter on the way.

I don't want to crush anybody's hopes and dreams; you might be a giant star one day, and once you're done rubbing it in my face I'd love to hear how fantastically things have worked out for you. To quote the lottery ads on TV 'It could be you!' And it could - *somebody* is going to get famous. There is a very good likelihood that several somebodies will get famous who you consider to be inferior musicians. People can seemingly get famous, and thus rich, for just about anything. Or indeed nothing. There is, however, nothing to stop you following the advice in this book to keep yourself dry in the rain until the fame train pulls up at your station!

Starting your Journey

Whether just leaving school or college, or looking to break from the world of work back to a passion lying dormant for many years, there is important groundwork to do to position yourself for success. I am not talking in the 'self-help' sense of positioning for success. I have never found looking in the mirror and screaming like a bear, or inventing my own 'I can, I must, I will, I am' reaffirmation mantra for the bathroom mirror every morning particularly helpful. If you do, then great, I'm sure you'll have time to fit that one in. But I'm speaking more of making success achievable.

When you think of being successful in the music business, what do you see? Swimming pools, champagne, houses in the country? Maybe the stereotypical fast cars and faster women? Well... I hope you get there. I assume you're reading this book because you're a fair distance away from that currently, and with that in mind we're going to start by being a little more modest in our expectations. Successes can be incremental, and milestones should be celebrated. I'll offer some for your consideration, but feel free to add your own:

★ Get your first paying job.

★ Make your first pound/dollar or equivalent from music.

★ Earn enough from music to go part-time at the day job.

★ Earn enough money to live from music alone.

★ Earn more from music than you do at your day job.

★ Earn enough from music to quit your day job.

★ Double your old day job income with music.

★ Become famous.

★ Quadruple your old day job income with music.

Only you can decide at what point you feel you will qualify as successful - it is extremely subjective. You may find your answer differs from that of your partner, your friends, your parents and the world at large. Some opinions may mean something to you, but the only one that counts is your own. Far and away the hardest hurdle to clear is the first, with everything following on from it. With consistent determination and application, there is no reason a job will not turn to money, just as there is no reason that your first paying job will not lead to more, allowing you to reduce time at the day job. As more work comes from referrals and you continue to explore the avenues this book will present, more money is a direct consequence. Match your salary, double it, who can say? Two thoughts should remain uppermost in your mind on this journey. Firstly, that meaningful success will be achieved when you can live off your income from music alone, though whether you choose to or not is entirely your decision. Secondly, that fame should be a by-product of being a capable music professional, held in high esteem by other music professionals and paying audiences. It can come in local, regional, national and international terms, but should not be anybody's goal starting out. If you work hard, are willing to keep an open mind when it comes to opportunity, and resilient in the face of failure, you will succeed.

If you start your journey with an expectation of a mansion on Richington Street, a Rolls Royce in the driveway, a Rolex on your wrist and a famous movie star on your arm by the end of year one, you may be headed for disappointment. In the same way, starting your journey handicapped by an enormous bag of debt on your back may also slow your ascent.

As you start planning your path to success in music, pay down your debts. Stop buying things on credit. Pay down and destroy your credit cards or at least keep them in a drawer for emergencies rather than a daily go-to. Other than a mortgage if you have one, your aim should be zero debt, and the approach is simple:

★ If you don't need it don't buy it.

★ If you do need it, pay cash and pay once - no instalments.

★ If you cannot afford it now, save for it.

Emergencies happen, and some expenses are unavoidable. If there is no alternative to taking credit, have a plan to pay it down BEFORE you take the debt. And stick to that plan to get back out of it. When you are responsible for your own success and your whole livelihood, you will feel the bad times as acutely as the good. Probably more so. It really helps to only have one debt to service rather than a number - both in terms of your available income and the amount of stress and anxiety that can result.

Be prepared to work longer hours initially. You may need to fit music work around your day job, which will mean evenings and weekends. Happily, the majority of strategies this book will explore are Internet-based and available 24/7, or leverage working practices that lend themselves well to a flexible and freelance approach. Hopefully, you will be able to go part-time pretty quickly and gradually wean yourself off a pay cheque, making it much easier to fit your developing new music career with your other commitments.

With my background in tech, I am an enormous fan of data. Statistics can frame things interestingly, and I believe they are a valuable tool for focussing the mind. Here are a few that I think relevant to somebody who thinks of 'making it big' when they think of success in music:

★ You have a 1 in 14million chance of winning the lottery.

★ You have a 1 in 55 chance of being a millionaire.

★ Your chances of being a billionaire? Around the same as your chance of being struck by lightning, and you don't want to be struck by lightning.

★ Your odds of being the next big thing are approximately 1 in 1.5million.

Clearly, money isn't the only measure of success. It probably isn't even the most important one. But that insight is much easier to embrace when you're neither cold nor hungry. You can see from the brief breakdown above though that chance alone is not in your favour, so you might not want to put all of your eggs in the 'making it big' basket.

The Plan - Foundation

So, what's the plan? I advocate working backwards: figure out what you need, then draw out a plan to achieve it. I have nominated £30K / $40K as an annual income I consider sufficient to live a happy life, all bills paid and enough spare for luxury items here and there. Your figure might be higher or lower. If higher, see the suggestion in the previous section on paying down debts and extend it to examining your outgoings for opportunities to reduce them, thereby maximising your potential for success. There are two ways to influence your level of success against an income benchmark. Clearly you could work hard and earn more money. You might also consider reducing the amount you need. Personally, I started by reducing my need and then worked on increasing my income. You can always buy a Porsche when you have the money, rather than worrying about how to make payments on the one in the driveway you can barely afford.

Let's assume that you're in work and/or education by way of 'day job', and your journey toward a successful music career starts today! Start by making a list for yourself and include the following:

- ★ How much money you need to live on
- ★ Expectations
- ★ Incremental achievements & milestones
- ★ Timescales
- ★ Skills (Music)
- ★ Skills (Other)
- ★ Your strengths to build on
- ★ Your weaknesses to overcome
- ★ Where you will find work, and who will help
- ★ Your audience

This initial assessment of the tools at your disposal is useful now to prompt possible affinity with some of the strategies that will follow over others. It may serve as motivation to see your strengths and skills listed. It will certainly frame the task at hand, and if you keep it somewhere as a reference point you can track your progress against it. You can also look back upon it in the future and see how far you have come. So, from the top.

How much money do you need to live?

The temptation is to frame this question in terms of what you currently earn or spend, because that has to be the amount you need to live, right? Well... sort of. It may well be an indication, but chances are you could live on less. You might think you can't live without three holidays abroad every year, and in the life you're leading now you might be right. But would you trade those holidays for being a successful music professional? You wouldn't be reading this if you wouldn't. Sacrifice is optional of course, and clearly you want to set your sights nice and high. But you can also cut yourself some slack and appreciate how attainable the ultimate dream is.

The majority of people could live on 10% less than their current income without even noticing. Buy your groceries at a cheaper supermarket, walk any journey that is less than a mile, stop buying £3 coffee from the chain coffee shops and so on. That same majority could live on over 15% less than their current expenditure. So undertake a review of your finances. Figure out your household necessities and be honest, what is a luxury to some could be a necessity to you, but in reality your mortgage/ rent, utility bills, taxes, and food are the only genuine necessities. So, the total for those items becomes the figure upon which you will have succeeded in music. Wow! That just got pretty real pretty quickly. And I'm betting it's suddenly a lot more possible than you thought, right?

Now, layer on the stages over and above the bare necessities. Maybe your next stage could be the bare necessities plus your mobile/ cell phone and your TV package. The one after that could be your current income. I think we all have to agree that achieving your current day job income with music would be one huge success - assuming of course that your day job now is covering your needs. And if not, all the more reason to get started!

As stated, we will be using £30K / $40K as the benchmark for a living, and I consider that to be a good living rather than scraping by. It was certainly good enough for me.

Expectations

There was a reason establishing the amount of money you need to live was the first item on the agenda. It would be easy to set yourself some pretty optimistic expectations from big houses and fast cars to quitting your job in the morning. With hard work we'll achieve everything in time, but it pays to start small.

Starting with more modest expectations brings achievement as close as possible, provides a much greater likelihood of success, and those early successes can be built on with ever-growing confidence. There are many people who will tell you to dream big, to make bold public statements regarding your success soon to come. I advocate a more reserved approach. Think of Scotty the chief engineer from Star Trek - who would say "I canna' do it captain!" in response to whatever ultimately life-saving challenge he was set. Or he'd tell Kirk it was going to take seven hours to complete a particular task, with the bad guys due to arrive in the intergalactic equivalent of 15 minutes. And then he went ahead and did it, against all the odds. Scotty was a hero. What if Scotty's line had been 'No worries captain, I can get that done in 5 minutes no problem!' If he managed it, fantastic - though he's also only done exactly what he said he'd do - no going above and beyond there. But if he still took the intergalactic 15 minutes, he'd appear a failure, and bye bye USS Enterprise!

The message here? Remain realistic in your assessments. Whether in your own mind or when speaking with others - avoid enthusiastic pronouncements of your new career direction. Not because it isn't exciting, we know it is. And not because you shouldn't have every faith in yourself, because you absolutely should. Communicating successes once achieved is much more satisfying than those yet to come. Partially because until the prize is in your grasp, it is too early to celebrate it, but much more pressing is the fact that by announcing a triumph on the horizon you completely rob yourself of the enjoyment derived from that moment of victory. So, do yourself a favour - delay that gratification. Keep your own expectations in check, and everybody else's will follow suit.

Incremental achievements & milestones

Related to the advice of the previous section to start small and keep a lid on your expectations, is the advice to give yourself some signposts along the way. If you're not making a penny from music right now, that first payment is a really big deal. You should feel proud of that. From there the path to day job salary replacement via music could be a long and winding one. Track all your payments - in a spreadsheet if you can, and on a piece of paper you keep somewhere safe if that's more your thing. Include who and what the job was, what it paid, how long it took and any expenses. When you start out I'd encourage taking any job that pays unless your opposition is well founded, since once you progress it will be helpful to know which jobs are worth most, and which customers are worth going back to. The answer on that, by the way, is probably all of them!

Keep a running total in your tracking system and establish how much your day job pays in a day, a week and a month. Keep in mind how much your rent and each major outgoing is. That way, you will know when your monthly music income reaches a level that matches a week of the day job, pays your electricity bill, bought groceries this week and so on. Moments like that can and will make all the hard work and perseverance worthwhile, and you'll be able to see success as a music professional coming in to sharper focus as the days roll by.

Not all milestones are monetary. Maybe you've been recording and sharing your music on various platforms for months and somebody just licensed a piece of your music - Fantastic! Perhaps you've been trying to land a writing job for an online magazine for ages, and the editor finally returned an email - Amazing! Again, keep note of all these breakthrough moments. Great for self-affirmation, as well as the encouragement to keep pushing forward in new directions. You've done it before; you can do it again!

Timescales

How quickly are you going to achieve success? This is another area where caution is advised. Clearly we would all like to be there already, if we really have to wait then maybe the end of the week or the end of the month is OK? I guess that depends on how driven you are and how badly you want to progress from existing circumstances.

It is wise to avoid statements like 'I will make all my money from music in x' amount of time. Obviously because the pressure you put on yourself is immense, and you're in danger of becoming the architect of your own failure. The reality here is that you haven't failed unless you give up - I am put in mind of the mantra of an athlete: 'fall down seven times, get up eight'. By all means set targets for your intermediate achievements and milestones, but think more in terms of the actions that advance them. So rather than 'I will have two composition commissions by the end of next month', perhaps 'I will have contacted five commissioning editors for TV and radio' is better. As a general rule, only set yourself targets and hold yourself to them if the entirety of the activity is within your control. You can commit to getting yourself to market, making a contact, finishing a lesson plan or book, but you cannot guarantee a paying customer.

I am sure, however, that you'd like some kind of an idea of what to expect from following the strategies in this book. Were I to tell you it will unfailingly take ten years to get to a meaningful income from music you might as well put the book down and go hunt down that promotion at the day job. I can tell you that my experience is that spending three months working extremely hard alongside the day job is likely, and should you manage to do that, there is no reason why an income from music should not be well underway. With that income from music, may come a re-evaluation of the day job. If you have a few early wins it could come very quickly, and if you're a bit unlucky you may only start seeing your efforts bear fruit toward the end of those three months.

It is then realistic to see the balance of your income shift from day job toward your new musical avenues over the course of the next six months. I am being deliberately conservative in my assessments because for one I can only comment on my own experience (I was done with my day job inside 6 months), and I've only just finished explaining that you shouldn't make any bold statements around timescales unless all the variables are within your control.

If you work hard, making a living from music in six months is completely achievable.

Skills (Music)

OK, so now we're getting into it. Let's assume that as you're reading a book on being successful in the music business without being a star, you have some background in music. You do? Phew! That could have been awkward, though based on many famous acts today you'd be forgiven for thinking musical skill was completely optional!

Give yourself an honest assessment of your skills with your primary instrument, and elements within the whole. Maybe you're a great pianist, but I bet some areas are stronger than others. Give yourself a score of five out of five for the element you feel is strongest, then give yourself a score out of five for the others using your best as a yardstick. Maybe you're a great sight reader but less good at improvisation. Perhaps you're good at Jazz but a lack-lustre Funk player. Try to think of as many categories as you can for as full a picture as possible, and don't award yourself full marks unless you genuinely feel you deserve them - this isn't a test nor a criticism, this is an honest assessment of where your skills and talents lie.

Now do the same with any secondary instruments or talents. Maybe you can't sing but you can manage an 'ooh', an 'aah' or a 'doo-wap' reasonably confidently, in time and in tune, whilst playing. Write yourself up as backing vocals and give yourself a score. Perhaps you've been recording yourself for years, and have developed skills in engineering and production with various sequencing products. A very significant strength in today's industry. Write it down.

Can you write music? Can you transcribe either from a TAB style notation to a score or from what you hear to a score? Fantastic - absolutely write that one down. Many musicians, myself included, have done extremely well for themselves with that particular skill. In the future you can use some of the material here to construct your music CV, minus the self-evaluation of course. In the meantime, this exercise has two purposes - to give you a view of how much you have to offer as a music professional and to highlight any areas of an emerging talent which could be built upon.

If your list feels a little light, do not despair. Go back to your list often, tweaking your scores and adding any new skills you acquire during your journey. We are also about to compliment your musical skills with your other talents.

Skills (Other)

We've covered your musical talents, now we need to consider your other skills and experience. Using the same method as before, give yourself five out of five for something you feel you're very good at and then score yourself against that baseline for everything else.

The day job is a good place to explore for this section. For example, I completed a literature degree and worked in information technology. So hopefully I'm a reasonably capable writer, and I can knock up a website. I've also run my own businesses over the years, which forces you to do a little bit of everything: a website, purchasing, stock management, photography, social media, customer services, marketing… you name it. Think laterally around everything you do in a typical day, and you'll be amazed what skills you use every day that transfer brilliantly to a career in music.

Extra points for any of the following, which will be massively useful in the coming pages:

★ Writing

★ Marketing

★ Social Media

★ Photography

★ Videography

★ Blogging

★ Computer literacy

If you spend a lot of your free time currently looking at a computer screen, or an iPad or similar, you're a lot more computer literate than I was way back when. We can and will be using those skills very soon, so it's worth breaking down further into software packages you are confident with and aspects of the Internet you understand. Maybe you already have a website. If you participate on social media you're already the curator of your own show, and we can build on that. These are real strengths, do not overlook them!

Your Strengths

Related to the above, yet distinct. Strengths might be personality traits such as versatility, flexibility, and perseverance. Are you able to try new things with a cheerful 'can do' sort of an attitude? Do you look like a musician? Are you confident in social situations? How about professional ones? Are you comfortable talking to a crowd? Do you have a lot of friends, and would you say people seem to like you? All these and many more are strengths well worth noting.

Resources would also be a strength - let's assume you have your own instruments and related equipment. Do you also have a car? A computer and an Internet connection? Access to a practice space or studio, however modest? A camera? All these could be enormously helpful. You need to be able to get to paying work or find a way to bring it to you.

Also, consider your current working situation and home life - these may belong here or in the next section. Do you have a job you can take time off from? An understanding boss? A supportive family? Being able to react to situations, as well as to work that may arise over time, will help you enormously. If any of these are a little lacking, no time like the present to set about fixing them. Be cautious. I am not suggesting you go ask your boss if he's cool with you trying to switch career, more suggesting you explore things like how many holiday days you've got left this year. Does your company have a sickness policy that permits a specific number of days off through illness whilst being paid? I'm not advocating the misuse of such an allowance of course, but knowing what it is can't hurt!

If your partner is somewhat doubtful of your new drive toward a music career, reassure them that it will not come at the expense of your day job, and that no risks are being taken. That this path is the one that resonates best with you, and that through hard work and determination you can enjoy your work and pay your way in the world. Genuine happiness is the pursuit here, not some frivolous dream. As you'll see from the facet-specific sections, there is some hard work ahead - no get rich quick promises!

Weaknesses

We all have weaknesses, there is no shame in them. In fact, an awareness of them could be considered a strength! I have already declared my shortcomings as a rhythm guitar player, and I explained that I make the best of that by incorporating my strengths. And therein lies the key - minimise the difficulties caused by any weaknesses by working in elements in which you excel.

Maybe you hate public speaking but you're a confident videographer. Well, there's a happy coincidence - you can film yourself speaking and use the video in lieu of personal appearance. You might also use the video as a memory aid for whatever you are planning to say, to critique your performance, or to deliver you to the realisation that although you might not enjoy it, you actually come across really well. You get the idea.

As a mirror opposite to the previous section, work, personal relationships and the absence of resources could be a weakness. No space to practice or record? Not ideal. No car? A significant limitation to the areas in which you can work and the ease with which you can get to them. If you are currently busy with a day job, consider prioritising some of your existing resources for such things. Modest investment is perfectly sensible. A car could be a necessity, and an additional amplifier plus a chair could be all it takes to turn your living room into a studio for teaching music lessons!

Weaknesses can, of course, be worked on. I don't have to stay a sub-par rhythm player. Equally, having achieved success where 'Rhythm Guitarist' was the job description, maybe I'm not as bad as I think I am. Maybe I'm only bad at that when I compare my rhythm performances to that in the area I feel strongest. In any event, identifying your weaknesses is the first step to addressing them, however you choose to do so.

Where will you find work, and who can help?

This section is about opportunities that already exist in your immediate vicinity. Keep your eyes and ears open as of right now for opportunities - I have gotten so much work from situations that might be seen as chance or blind luck. I'm not sure I believe in luck, but either way you can improve your chances.

When you're out socialising, be aware of venues that include live music, and make a note. Particularly solo performers. Do you have kids in a local school? If so, you're on the front foot with a whole bunch of potential customers in the other children and their parents. At work, I bet if you've been listening you already know at least one person who would like lessons in an instrument in which you're proficient.

Getting on the front foot is key here. As you plan your move away from the day job and toward music, use all the opportunities you have. Put up a card on the staff noticeboard for piano lessons, speak with any colleagues who sound in the market for lessons. Should any of your co-workers declare themselves as musicians, exchange contact details and make sure to get in touch outside of a work context. These people already know you well, and can vouch for you as a trustworthy and dependable person (assuming you are one!) Even if they cannot speak to your prowess in music, we all know people prefer to take recommendations from those they trust. Your next job could come from the people sat around you right now.

Are you active in the music scene at all? Add signing up to Internet forums relevant to your specific instrument, favoured musical genres and wider interests to your 'things to do right now' list. There are hundreds of them out there, some better travelled than others. A quick Internet search will offer up your best options. Once you have signed up, drop in an introduction post, have a look around and see whether there are any discussions you feel you want to get involved with. It isn't considered good manners to dive straight in with pitching your services, so start gently and make some new contacts.

If you are not already very aware of how true the old adage "It's not what you know, it's who you know" is, you will very soon find out. As soon as you're relying on yourself for your next pay cheque, you'll be grateful for every friend you have. Think of networking as a complex favour system - building relationships with others for mutual benefit. Make sure you help others freely and often if you expect the same by return.

I cannot overstate this enough - I got, and continue to get, a significant portion of my work from people I already know, people I have worked with and my various social circles. It truly is a small world.

I've mentioned my music teacher previously, and his insights have been vital to my development as a music professional. I have always taken lessons weekly; beyond all the formal examinations I have submitted myself for. It keeps me engaged, maintains my talents with an instrument, drives me to improve and, perhaps most importantly, gives me the opportunity to work with others more established than I in the local music community. Such people are invaluable. Each full-time music tutor is likely to have thirty or more students, and whilst it would be bad manners to attempt to tempt away any of them, those links could help you in future. As I've mentioned, I get a great deal of work from people I know.

Always be alert to opportunity. I got my first theatre job from a chance conversation on a train. When people are having those 'so what do you do?' conversations, everybody gets really interested really fast when you respond with "I'm a musician". I walked away from one of those conversations with a phone number which I called the following day and ended up playing in a major London theatre several nights a week. That job alone would have met the 'matching your day job salary' success test all on its own!

Who is your audience?

This question merits extensive thought. You might substitute it with 'who are my customers?' these are the people you want to connect with as a music professional - other musicians, producers, business owners, teachers, potential students, writers, studio owners... the list is endless. Engagement comes later, but identification can start right away.

You need to start thinking of yourself as a musician - as a brand. Start using your voice as a musician to let people know you're there. As suggested in the previous section, make sure you're always aware of those around you, ready for that half comment or opening that gives you an 'in'. If you've taken the advice in the previous section to join some appropriate forums, get with the networking. Reach out to people, answer questions, become known as an expert in your field. It is not difficult to become a decent sized fish in a pond, and hopefully you've already got that underway.

Set up a website (more on that later!), and use the address in emails and forum signatures so it accompanies every post. Use your website address on social media and video or image sharing sites... everywhere. The more people see it; the more people will interact with you. The more it is written down, the easier it is for search engines to find and prioritise you. As a modern music professional with access to the Internet, the answer to the 'Who is your audience?' question is 'Everyone'. Worldwide. Language is a barrier to an extent, at least in terms of engagement, but music is pretty universal. Do not close yourself off to any avenue, because all avenues mean opportunity.

There are several likely opportunities available to you with every single person you ever meet. Without knowing a person well, you can already be certain they have a birthday every year. You can be reasonably confident that either they or somebody they know is getting married soon - and straight away there are possibilities for a performance booking. Maybe they have children, or showed an interest in your chosen instrument? Well, there's an opportunity to tell them it isn't that hard if they have a good tutor... and did they know you are a tutor? Well, there's a coincidence. Only it isn't a coincidence, merely a fact of life. In a continuation of previous thoughts, the majority of the people you meet will have friends, family, and co-workers who participate in music somehow, or wish they did. And a connection through a mutual friend will get your foot in the door.

Once you start getting work, publicise your successes on your new website. Then as your circle of contacts, or 'audience', grows you can ensure they're all up to date with what's new with you, as well as how they can be a part of it.

Onward, to Success!

O K, this is where we start making progress. In the sections that follow we will sketch out several areas in which working musicians are successful today, and opportunities where there is more than enough work to go around.

Each section includes a five-point scale for each of the following: difficulty, cost, time commitment, the likelihood of success and income potential. Any required or beneficial resources will also be included. And since I have personally used these strategies I will provide real-world facts and figures to back them up, giving you a realistic view of not only what is possible, but what is realistic based on the recent experience of somebody in a similar position to you. You will very quickly see how possible that music career you thought was beyond your grasp has become.

The sector-specific sections can be read in any order since they are completely separate. If you are interested in teaching, head for that section. Writing, get yourself to that section. Likewise, the performance, recording, Internet... and so on. Please do eventually visit all of them though, since there are so many branches of music you could embrace to increase your success; it would be a shame to close any of them off.

Finally, I will stitch together my own experience of doing this full-time to show how the various income streams can build, as well as working together to increase income from all directions. My annual income from music is triple the income from my last salaried job, and although I am now some ten-years removed from that day job, I hit the two-fold salary multiplier after around 3 years. You may recall we discussed motivation previously, and how my ultimate motivation for all this hard work was eventually to be in a position where I could stop doing the day job? Well, I am now in the same situation as my teacher all those years ago who, fully committed, offered additional work to me. I now happily recommend people on a similar path, knowing that feeding and watering those relationships is probably the single best investment I can make in my professional future.

There are no get rich quick schemes, scams, tricks or secrets in the pages that follow, just genuine advice from somebody who has done it before, and has managed to be successful in the music business, making money without being a star!

Your own Internet site

Overview

★ ★ ★ ☆ ☆   Difficulty

★ ★ ☆ ☆ ☆   Cost

★ ★ ★ ☆ ☆   Time Commitment

★ ★ ★ ★ ★   Likelihood of Success

★ ★ ★ ★ ★   Income Potential

Required resources: Your choice - either the skills to create your own, time to acquire them or the means to pay somebody else to provide it for you!

This section is up first because it links all the others together, and you will find elements of all the sections that follow tying back to a simple core truth. You need your own Internet site. In seeking to make money in the music business, people need to know you are there. You could sit in your living room and declare yourself a professional musician today, but if nobody knows you, you are unlikely to be successful. The single easiest and most cost-effective thing you can do is get yourself a website set up. There are hundreds, probably thousands, of companies that can assist you in this effort, and you can pay pretty much anything from a few hundred pounds to several thousand, but it is preferable to do it all yourself - from the point of view of cost obviously, but also as you're going to want to update it frequently to keep your audience engaged. If you are not in a position to do it yourself, you will be at a significant disadvantage.

This is **ABSOLUTELY** the single most important component of your plan for success. Start work today. Investing money is wise, and if not possible due to circumstances, investing time is strongly advised. The skills required are easy to acquire, and tools are available to make it as easy as using a word processor or email system. Your own website links together everything you do as a music professional and allows you to multiply revenue streams and cross-sell with ease.

OK - From the top:

Domain Names

You will need a www.something.something address for people to type in when they're looking for you. The .com variants are the most popular, and the geographical options come in second. The geographical domains like .co.uk are helpful in some respects since although you could be global in reach, anybody wanting to secure your services will be grateful for an indication of where in the world you are.

Though it may be tempting to name your business 'blue krab muzik', think carefully. That particular bad example is bad for the following reasons:

★ It doesn't tell anybody very much about the business

★ The words are unrelated, making it difficult to recall

★ 'krab' and 'muzik' are spelled incorrectly

And that last bullet is the real problem here. Were you to name your business something like that, you're going to find yourself explaining every time you say it that "that's 'crab' with a 'k' and 'music' with a 'z' and a 'k'". That's every single time you want to tell somebody your website address or email. And that's going to get old really fast. It might also not land well with the person you're attempting to explain it to. Resulting in them losing interest.

So, go with your own name if possible. More difficult if you're a 'John Smith', but maybe it is also an opportunity to rock and roll it up a bit and become a 'Jonno Smith', 'Smithy Johns' or similar. You might also consider adding your preferred instrument to the domain name, or 'music' after your name. If you must name your business something you consider clever or imaginative, at least spell all the component words correctly to save people guessing. In the early days you will be lucky if someone tries to send you an email once. If they cannot easily enter your email address at that first time of asking, you might not get a second chance.

You really cannot access the Internet today without stumbling over companies that will register a domain for you left and right. Make sure you read the terms and conditions carefully - some of the organisations that will register a name for you for free or for a few pennies only offer that service to entice you into additional services. Some retain ownership of the domain, most will oblige you to use their services to design and/ or hold the website for you at additional cost. These things are not necessarily a problem, but it is important you understand what you are agreeing to - particularly as once the domain is registered via such a company, there is no way to release it from their terms and conditions.

Hosting

Once you have secured a domain name, you need a place to park it. This is known as hosting, and will typically be expressed in terms of disk space and bandwidth. Should you be in the market for these things, compare available offerings and choose one that fits your budget - none will be very expensive. Email will be included in this setup, so once you have asked a company to host your domain for you, someone wishing to send an email to you will be able to, though a bit more work is needed for a functional website.

Design

This section is where the real work is, and there is more than sufficient material on website design to create books on this subject alone. As many people have. From the point of view of a musician who needs a website, there are several shortcuts available that will make the creation of a website quicker, easier and cheaper.

Not so long ago, if you wanted to build a website you would need to master several flavours of code, HMTL being the one you have most likely already heard of. Now, if you wanted to embrace my philosophy and learn to do everything yourself in pursuit of being a rounded professional, you could be looking at several months of reading, experimenting, and in all likelihood eventually building a website that you're not happy with anyway. You could, of course, be using that time more profitably and interestingly on practicing your instrument, or on one or more of the many strategies that follow. Unless you want to become successful in the website design business without becoming a star, I recommend you give that one a miss. Fortunately for us all, there are loads of options available to you that will make it possible to design your website without learning any code at all!

The Easy Option

Content Management Systems, known henceforth as CMS, have completely revolutionised the business of building a website. Moving the enterprise from professional design outfits to become achievable to anyone with a few hours to spare. That's not to say you wouldn't get a better result from a design studio, which you very likely would… but you would also have to pay for that privilege. A CMS driven website could be up and running in around an hour.

At the time of writing, WordPress powers around 50% of the sites you see on the internet, and it has several advantages:

★ It is free

★ It is easy to install

★ It is easy to customise, with FREE templates available

★ It is easy to update, very much like a word-processing software package

★ It is responsive - so will display well on mobile devices and tablets

★ It has plugins for any function you want

You will have noticed how often I mentioned it being easy, because it really is easy. I suffered the pain and anguish of learning some HTML to build my own website many years ago. Whilst part of me would like to talk you into doing the same, as it's what my Dad would call 'character building', it is also a massive pain in the ass and I cannot in good conscience suggest you do anything other than installing WordPress. Once you have found an Internet hosting company, it is all but certain they will provide you with the means to install WordPress with a click of a button. You will be asked for basic configuration details including usernames and passwords. Please write them down somewhere, because 1) you're going to need them and 2) it would be a real shame to be locked out of your own website!

Once you have installed WordPress you will need a template. There are several built into the installer, most of which are inoffensive and ready to go. There are also template sites accessible via your favourite search engine that can provide you with templates tailored to your needs for minimal cost (around £50). For a few pounds more they will install them for you as well, though the process is far from difficult. Pretty much all you need in either event is a logo and some content. That logo could be anything right now: perhaps a photo you have taken, a royalty-free image from the internet or something custom. There are many freelancer sites where you will be able to find someone to put together a simple logo for you for the price of a cup of coffee - I recommend that approach since it means you get something unique to you.

Armed with some hosting, some WordPress, and a template, we're on to content. The basics will be:

★ Contact details.

★ A 'Bio' section, about you.

★ Some pictures of you in action.

★ Details of services: teaching, session playing etc.

Websites today typically feature video, either within the site or linked from video sharing platforms, and social media links for people to interact with content. Use them if you can; the more means you have at your disposal to engage with your audience, the more chance you have of paid work happening by.

There will be more later in this section on content, and on making your content friendly to search engines. This will make them rank you higher, making it more likely that people searching for a musician with your skills will find you, but for now, note that the more often you update your site the better from a search point of view. So, include work you are doing, performance dates, updates on teaching - basically anything relevant to your music career that you believe your audience would like to read about. Up to date website content shows the world you are actively working in music, and gives the impression of someone who is engaged and passionate about their work.

The Easiest Option

Though WordPress has made the creation of a top-quality website a realistic proposition for you, me and anyone else with basic computer skills, there is an even easier option - redirection. With a handful of clicks, you could save all the website creation stuff full stop and get on with your music business.

From within your hosting service, your domain name can be configured to redirect to another site, so you could simply set it up to do that. Once redirection is enabled, anybody clicking on www.yourwebsite.com could be directed to www.yoursocialmediasite.com/yourpage. This provides a very quick and easy means to display something legible and easily navigated to your audience, though it will be apparent to anyone viewing that the content is nothing more than your page in social media. If you go with this option, make sure you complete sections in social media for contact details and the 'about' section. Keep in mind that this information needs to be fully public for anyone and everyone to be able to access it. This may make creating a second profile an attractive option, so you can ensure you only share information you want to be available to everyone on your professional social media presence. This is a good idea in general since it prevents any potentially embarrassing content shaping the impression your audience receives.

Putting together your own site is a much better solution for your business as it gives a much more professional impression to your website, but as a strictly short-term measure, redirection of your domain to social media, video sharing or similar is acceptable. It should not be considered an option longer term, since in today's music world your audience will expect any professional organisation or individual to have their own website, properly and professionally structured.

Content

Clearly, if you're going to the trouble of having a website with the notion of attracting paid work, it makes sense to list the specialisms for which you are available. This clearly will be driven by which elements in the rest of this book you choose to pursue. The core of the site remains as indicated previously: you need a biography section, a contact section and a bit of style around the piece generally, but beyond that, you need to prioritise content as you see fit and in line with the work you are seeking.

A Home Page

Your home page is the first page people will see when visiting www.yourwebsite.com. It is important you make a good initial impression so they are inclined to browse the site and learn more. Make sure the structure is clear and uncluttered, and that links to sections you want people to see are easy to find. If you are running a blog or 'news' section you will want that to appear prominently, along with any releases of new material or upcoming gigs. It is good to start with a few options and allow them to develop; a long list of links would not be recommended!

About

It really helps drive business to get your audience (or customers!) to engage with you as an individual. You need to craft an image, and whilst that image should be of a capable professional musician, it also doesn't hurt to let them know a bit about you. Maybe you drive an old car, maybe you've got a scruffy looking dog, a passion for [insert kooky thing here] - it doesn't really matter. You might not feel comfortable divulging something *really* personal, and indeed it might not be appropriate for you to do so, but making people feel they know you will make them feel at ease. And people like working with people they like. So, use your 'About' page to help them get to know you.

Gallery

An extension of the previous section really. If you want people to know what you're about and feel they know you, they need to be able to see you. Preferably in a music context: playing live, practicing, or teaching a lesson. Maybe some arty shots of you sat with your preferred instrument in a bar, coffeehouse or next to a river. It doesn't matter too much, but be mindful these shots are the image you are projecting to the world. Think about where you are and what you are doing and ensure your pictures reflect your intentions. Make sure as well that they are in focus and adequately composed. They do not need to be professionally done, but making sure everything you want to have in shot, is in the shot, is a solid place to start!

Contact

It would be a shame to go to the trouble of having a website and filling it with loads of interesting information, and then not providing means for people to get in touch. Having a contact page is pretty much obligatory for a website today. There are several CMS plugins available to automate this, and all you'll need is an email address for website contacts to be sent to. Make sure to include opportunities for those contacting you to let you know how to get back to them. It may sound ridiculous, but I know plenty of people who lost business because they couldn't return a contact. As an extension of the thought, make sure you set an expectation on the page for how long it will take you to reply, and then do your very best to reply within that timescale. You want to look engaged and interested in those who are interested in you.

Music

The presence of this section on a musician's website should come as no surprise! You are going to want recordings of you in action so fans, friends and potential customers can see what you're about. The content of this section should be driven by your aspirations more widely. If you're selling lessons, an excerpt of one would provide a useful insight. If you're selling a record, some tracks from it would help. Function performances? Some stock repertoire perhaps. It is a good idea to provide a mixture to showcase your versatility, and to demonstrate your range as a musician. If you show a dozen death metal pieces and nothing else, you may find it as much of a struggle to get a gig at a local Catholic school as you would trying to get a death metal gig off the back of a collection of hymn instrumentals. So, keep it eclectic.

A Shop

A shop inventory will be driven by the services you offer really. It might include CDs, T-Shirts and stickers, books, video lesson downloads, links to download music from the various digital platforms and so forth. It might also include gift cards redeemable for lessons or personalised songs such as birthday greetings, and once you are a little more established a site membership subscription is also plausible, though you would need frequently updated material and a 'members' section to justify it. It is a great idea to list products and services that you could provide so that in the event somebody is looking for that service, they can see you provide it. It would be a shame to lose business because a visitor to your site didn't see a button for 'personalised Christmas greetings' for instance. There is a happy medium - you're not going to want to list everything you can think of, but having a browse around the Internet to see what the competition is doing is always a sensible place to start!

Your shop could also contain affiliate links, which are a way for you to sell items without holding stock or processing orders. Several of the large online retailers offer affiliate programs which you can join, and they will provide instructions for listing products. Should a visitor to your site purchase one of these products, you'll get a commission paid. It is good manners to announce this behaviour on your site, but provided you sell items that are related to your field, and that you personally would recommend, I believe you can do so without compromising your artistic integrity! Music sales sites such as CDBaby, iTunes, and Amazon all offer affiliate services, and Musician's Friend offer the same for musical instrument sales. As a fledging music professional, you can and will find that all these opportunities for pennies can add up quickly into a respectable income. Do not turn your nose up to any of them until you have the luxury!

Driving Traffic

Now that you've got a website, you want people to see it. There are two basic paths that will deliver your audience to your site: Search Engines and Social Media.

Search Engines

We all have our 'go to' search engine, and their methods for matching content to searches are essentially the same. Being mostly automated, search engines examine sites to determine what they are about, and do so by processing the words appearing within. So, if you would like to be returned as an option for a search on clarinet players in Cincinnati, you will want to work into your site that you are a clarinet player in Cincinnati. Probably repeatedly. 'Clarinet Player Cincinnati' is a keyword in search engine terms, and appearing in searches for a particular word or phrase requires repetition. This may call for slightly inelegant writing on your part, tailored for a robotic audience as well as the human one. There are several things that you can do easily to maximise your potential:

★ Use your keyword or phrase as a heading (or part of a heading) on the page.

★ Use your keyword or phrase a few times within the text, naturally if possible.

★ Keep your page to around 400 words in length - hitting the sweet spot between being long enough to merit a visit but short enough to maintain interest.

★ Keep sentences short and sweet, around 20 words is good where possible.

★ Do not work with the same keyword or phrase on more than one page - you want people to go to your site but to some extent it doesn't matter which page they land on.

★ Use 'Alt' tags for images on the page that include the keyword or phrase.

As you might imagine for an industry that has spawned a profession dedicated to it, search engine optimisation can be a complicated beast, and if you really want to rank very high in searches your best bets are to pay an expert to help you, or pay the search engine company for advertising to come out top. The above is a very good start for making your own content as accessible as possible though.

One area many musicians starting out overlook is making sure their own name is properly listed by search engines. In the early days, this does not help traffic to your site of course since you are not well known enough to be a search term. You are, however, building a brand as a musician, and that process starts on day one. If people are looking for clarinet players in Cincinnati and they start finding Ms. Clara Net, you want them to associate the name with the act. So make sure you mention your name (or working name if more appropriate) on your homepage regularly.

As mentioned previously, it is also important to update your site regularly. Search engines will refer their users to content they judge valuable, interesting and current. If you update your site regularly the search engines will know it is worth directing people toward your site. The 'Interesting' judgement is arrived at via the automated processing of text for keywords as explained, the final 'Valuable' component is derived from the volume of traffic hitting your website already, which you can do little to influence in the very early days. Except of course that you can!

Social Media

Assuming you already have an Internet presence in the form of social media accounts, start telling your friends and work colleagues about your new site as soon as possible. Plug it whenever there is something new there to check out. Don't overdo it and alienate your potential audience, but take advantage of those already interested in you and your musical journey. Linking via social media, in video and in forum signatures has been mentioned elsewhere. Include a link to www.yoursite.com whenever you are talking in a public Internet location as your musician persona. Doing so creates what are known as 'backlinks' - links to your site from other sites. These are another mechanism search engines use to establish how useful and interesting your site is likely to be to a wider audience.

Integrate your social media presences with your website by adding functionality for the familiar 'like' and 'share' options prevalent across the Internet. Include links to your social media sites on your website, if necessary setting up additional pages separate from your personal ones. Keep the pictures of your lunch and the 'funny' cat pictures on your personal pages, and the music on your musician pages - you want to build a professional presence. We're back to brand. Include the address for your website on everything you can. Digitally on social media, forums and all other websites. In print on CD sleeves, T-Shirts, flyers, images used for digital downloads. In the title sequence for shared video. You name it, if there is any opportunity to get your name out there, take it.

Maintaining a Profile

For all the reasons above, when pursuing, progressing and maintaining a successful career as a musician you do not need to be a star, but you do need to maintain a presence. Establishing a brand has been mentioned, creating a persona has been mentioned. Giving people an insight into you, your life and personality and allowing them to get to know you in some measure has been mentioned. We have explained the simple concept that people are more likely to work with or spend money with, people they like. Which restaurant would you eat at given the choice of:

 A nice place with courteous staff selling decent food, or;

 A rundown joint with rude staff, selling good food.

The first one for sure. If the food was truly incredible you might overlook other shortcomings of the second option, but the greater the shortcomings the better the food needs to be. And if the shortcomings are evident from a distance, would you ever have been brave enough to go in and order, then find out the food is amazing? Probably not. And it is the same for you as a musician. The impression you give via your website and social media can get you work as easily as it can lose you work.

Make sure your website is as polished as it can be. If you want to do everything yourself, or cannot afford professional assistance, at least ask a friend or relative to give it a once over click-around. Make sure the buttons work, the spellings are correct, and that everything a viewer might need is accessible. Make sure videos are well produced, and that the sound quality of recordings is acceptable.

Make sure your social media profiles are kept up to date with material suitable to your professional presence and make sure to plug your website every opportunity you get. Even adding a signature to emails that includes a logo and a link to your website can get you traffic from the recipient of that email. Seriously, never miss an opportunity. People know people, so get your name out there every chance you get.

Monetising

It is possible to get your own website generating revenue in several ways. An online shop could make money and downloads of songs will make money, but one of the best ways to generate a steady income is advertising. It will not pull in a fortune unless you get really serious traffic volumes, but it is another one of those things that takes seconds to set up and can make you a few pounds/dollars here and there, which contribute to your greater goal of success for zero effort going forward. And that is exactly the kind of income we're looking for!

There are several players in the paid advertising market, most of them being the major players in the search engine market. Businesses pay the search companies to advertise their services, and the search providers, as a result, need sites willing to display those ads. The search engines take the advertising money, pay an amount of it to those willing to host the ads and keep the difference between the two. To make money from advertising on your website, you will need people to visit your site, and ideally to click on the adverts themselves. You will get a few pennies for each visitor to your site, a view of an advert is called an impression, and a few more pennies should a site visitor click on the advert. If you get to the point of generating thousands of visitors per day, you can make tens of pounds from advertising each day, which soon mounts up to a decent annual figure.

You may need to meet certain qualifying criteria for the advertising companies, specifically you will need the home, about and contact pages we have discussed previously. You will also need a privacy page that talks about how your site uses the viewer's personal information. This is because the advertisers use little snippets of code, called cookies, to note what sort of topics a person searches for, and use that data to display relevant ads to them. Once you have those pages, and an amount of content a viewer would find engaging, apply for the advertising programs. Once accepted, you will be provided with the code to add to your website, and instructions with which to complete the necessary steps. It literally takes a few minutes, and as I have explained, could make you money every day afterwards for literally no effort at all.

Many website owners also accept payment for reviews of items on their site. This is your call, and it is a revenue stream, but my belief is that accepting payment for a review could give rise to a suspicion of the payment being motivation for the positivity of a review. I feel it undermines the integrity of a site, and perhaps of recommendations in general. Can a site visitor trust what you're saying if you are being paid to say it? That particular avenue isn't for me, but I'm sure if you were upfront with your audience about the paid nature of the review it could work, and it is certainly lucrative.

Potential Income

It could be argued that your website will contribute directly to almost all income you derive from music, that people in search of a music professional will find you because of your site, and potential customers wanting to find out more about you will do so via your site. It is priceless in that respect, and it is vital you do a good job of it. It is your shop front; a showcase for your talents.

Once your website is well established, you could easily make £20 per day from it in advertising revenue, a figure I am basing on a site of mine that attracts around five hundred visitors per day. With a solid social media following and regular updates, this is completely achievable and the estimate is a conservative one. You could drive much more traffic to your site, and make much more from advertising revenue as a result.

An affiliate store will again make you an income based on site visitor activity. If you are linking CDs, music instruments and similar equipment it is not unreasonable to expect a similar income from the affiliate store to the online advertising. My experience has been that the affiliate store is comparable in terms of income, but it is reliant on your site visitors having some faith in your point of view. I truly only list items in my stores that I use myself, and I do not accept payment for reviews as explained above.

There is a separate section devoted to the sale of your music, so I will cover income from recorded works there, indicative income from your website for the purposes of this section being confined to monies made from the site itself rather than the sale of other items it enables.

Real world example

I have many websites, but only update a couple of them regularly. Both of these run custom advertising programs and one has an affiliate store selling music-related equipment which I use myself. I do not go out of my way to advertise the items, but they are items I genuinely use myself, and that appear in my videos. This is not product placement or a deliberate strategy; I am making available the gear I use myself and would happily recommend to a friend, student or family member. My current income from a single site is as follows:

Advertising (Annual)	£5200
Affiliate Store (Annual)	£5200
Total	**£10400**
Having a website as a Pro Musician	Priceless!
Time Spent (Weekly)	~2hrs*

Which means an income from websites of around **£100 per working hour**, plus all the benefits of having the website to drive business more generally!

The advertising revenue is completely passive; it is zero effort once the initial setup is complete.

* Initial site setup took more time - the evenings of a week specifically. This was not time that cost me money as such but it did eat into my TV watching! Once the site was set up, 2 hours per week is sufficient for a handful of updates per week on various subjects, as well as infrequent additions to the store and so on.

Tuition

Overview

★ ★ ☆ ☆ ☆   Difficulty

★ ☆ ☆ ☆ ☆   Cost

★ ★ ★ ★ ★   Time Commitment

★ ★ ★ ★ ★   Likelihood of Success

★ ★ ★ ☆ ☆   Income Potential

Required resources: available time, a suitable venue, necessary equipment (a piano for piano lessons, and extra amplifier for guitar lessons etc.)

Tuition does not have to be difficult. If you are a competent musician you already have the basic skills required. If your living room has your chosen instrument and a spare chair you have the bare necessities covered.

It is said that an individual need only know one thing more than their student to be a successful tutor, and whilst that might be true, strictly speaking, it will not make you a good tutor. You need to have a competence in your instrument sufficient to confidently guide someone else. If you are not quite that well advanced in your own talents, you can address this by being selective in those you teach. You could, for instance, only teach true beginners. Take them through the first three grades on the piano for example. In so doing you would build your teaching experience and buy time to build your capabilities, whilst earning a solid income. You might also consider playing to your personal strengths and teaching a specific aspect of an instrument - jazz improvisation for example. Doing so would allow you to focus on technique and helping a student build their chops, rather than ask difficult theory questions of you week on week. There are several avenues within tuition that are worth exploring.

Face to face lessons

The bread and butter staple of a music tutor: traditional one to one lessons. Typically offered in 30-minute, 45-minute or one-hour variants. Personally, I find 30 minutes is too short to provide meaningful results. If a student is motivated by a reduction in cost, participating in a group lesson would likely work better for them. The decision point on duration between 45 minutes and an hour is largely a personal one. The 45-minute option gives you turnaround time between students but may mean a decrease in income. The best idea frankly is to see what all the other tutors in your area are doing, and do the same; that will be what your customer base expects.

Be mindful that your audience for lessons requires a means to pay for them, and hence are likely to be working during the day. Younger students may well be at school. The majority of students either way will be occupied on weekdays until 3:30pm or later. This may result in your having to work hours you would have previously considered 'unsociable': evenings and weekends. To build a full-time teaching week could well mean working between 3pm and 7pm on weekdays, as well as some portion of the weekends. The retired community is an obvious exception, and many people in later life enjoy taking on new hobbies.

You will need a room that is as quiet as possible, with chairs suitable for the task for both yourself and your student. Appropriate provision for instruments is an obvious requirement: a piano for piano lessons, an extra amplifier so both of you can plug in for guitar lessons, and so on. A music stand is a must, as is a reliable means of tuning if students are bringing their own instruments to lessons. It is extremely difficult to teach without distraction if the instruments are not either in tune, or at least in tune with each other. You will benefit from a notepad to offer notes to your student, and lesson plans can be enormously helpful.

As a shortcut on lesson planning when starting out, buy the grade books for all grades up to two below your highest achieved. If you have not undertaken formal examinations, take a look at the content and aim two below the limit of your confidence. This should mean that you're dealing with material you're comfortable with. The books serve several purposes:

★ They provide the student with confidence they are following a proven path

★ They provide opportunity for exam preparation - another income stream

★ They provide an ongoing lesson plan

★ They provide easy evidence of progress for students and their parents

So, for a novice tutor, or a more experienced one with exam success as an agenda, the grading system as it exists is a fantastic framework to start with. Feel free to augment it, particularly including pieces that use the skills acquired in a more 'pop' context. Many of the grading syllabuses are famously dry, with chords, scales, and arpeggios aplenty. But often not a great deal of fun in application.

Standard one to one lessons are entirely reliant on your time, and the income derived from them is linked directly to the amount of time you spend delivering them. This is a positive in so far as working harder will deliver a healthier income but a negative in requiring your time to be occupied by teaching lessons. However, a foothold in teaching is extremely positive overall; you will improve as a musician and you will future-proof your business to some extent.

One cannot complete a music education - there is always more to learn. And provided you stay ahead of your students, you could be there to guide them throughout their journey.

Making yourself known to customers is also straightforward. For all avenues explored a website is recommended; please review that section for more information if you have not done so already. List lessons on your own website using a calendar showing your availability if possible. You might also consider joining professional teaching bodies and directories for greater exposure. This is a minimal expense for instant access to hundreds of potential customers - and you only need a couple of dozen! You can also print leaflets, business cards, and contact local schools to offer enhancements to their music programs.

On that final point, being approved by a relevant authority is helpful. In the UK this is the Disclosure and Barring Service, or DBS. The organisation will check your criminal record, and being issued with a check number indicating your previously good character is extremely helpful. It is mandatory for work in schools and will ease the fears of many parents considering entrusting their child to your care.

Income from teaching is relatively secure, though you should be mindful of the possibility of students going on holiday, your income's vulnerability to illness (since if you can't teach you will not get paid) and the bugbear of every music tutor: the no-show. Students just not attending lessons without notice. Threats of charging regardless are common, but falling out of favour with a student could hit revenue for much more than a single missed lesson. A judgement made case by case is advised, since teaching is almost as reliant on relationship building as it is on your skill as a musician.

Group Lessons

Group lessons are very effective as an income generator. Six students in a one-hour session will be more lucrative than one, and generally the cost to the individual student is reduced, making them desirable to the student as well. The challenge here is essentially two-fold: firstly, can you accommodate a class rather than a single student? Secondly, have you access to a group of suitable size, the members of which are all of similar ability?

The solution to both difficulties can be found in the same place. Group classes should be sought in places where groups often congregate: schools, community groups, perhaps even workplaces as team building opportunities. Finding six people individually, all of whom are zero-experience beginners, and all of whom are available on Tuesday at 6pm is probably as close to impossible as you'll ever want to get. Finding an organisation who can provide just such an audience to you in one move is significantly more likely, as well as being easier for all concerned. It is also likely that the organisation in question will have a suitable venue for the classes to take place.

If you are interested in exploring group lessons, approaching local schools, community groups and businesses is the best first step. There are also a number of companies on the Internet specialising in organising corporate events, and a group 'rock star experience' day would be an easy sell. It would be very achievable to charge in excess of £100 per hour for a group lesson. Although you would need to take account of travel time, any expenses incurred in that travel can usually be added to your bill.

Other than that, all the observations for individual lessons in the previous section still apply. Use the grade books as a starter to plan and conduct lessons, as well as tracking and demonstrating progress. You may find group lessons are useful during a more traditional working day - if teaching in a school, clearly you will be working in the school day, possibly over a lunch hour. Group lessons such as these can be a very useful income boost in what otherwise could be not very well utilised time.

Online Lessons

The Internet has revolutionised the world of work, and music is no exception. Where the horizons of a tutor used to be limited to his or her immediate area, students can now be sought worldwide, and lessons conducted without anyone leaving their home.

Slightly more equipment is required; essentially a computer, a webcam, a microphone and some sort of means to communicate with your student. Armed with those and a suitable studio environment, you're ready to do lessons online! There are some logistical challenges to overcome:

★ Will the student arrive on time?

★ Will the Internet connection hold up well enough for video?

★ Will the student's instrument be in tune, and;

★ Will they be able to tune it themselves?

And of course many more, but the advantages are also significant. You will have no travel time, and neither will your student - and it is this which makes geography an irrelevance. You can overcome the challenge of having people you don't know visiting your home, at the same time eliminating the risks to them associated with an unknown person. It is possible to record lessons conducted in this way, and doing so may be wise, both from the point of view of having a record of performance but also for your own protection. If any questions arise around your conduct, you will have an audio record of what transpired in a lesson, as well as video of one or both sides, depending on configuration. The software will advise participants that they are being recorded, but make sure all parties understand recording is happening, and that it is for mutual benefit.

There are several software packages that are free to use and allow video calling, which may be sufficient for starting out with online teaching. There are also premium services that offer video lesson services, scheduling with calendar, tracking of assignments, practice schedules, and payments - essentially everything you need to run an online tuition business. As always, your favourite search engine will deliver appropriate results where necessary, and links to appropriate resources can be found on www.mmimusicbooks.com.

The lesson is only half the transaction, of course. Having touched on payments we should address how these can be handled minus face to face interaction. Direct bank deposits are available. They may even be preferable from the point of view of convenience as well as the commission fees some payment processing services charge.

However, these are riskier from a customer point of view as they are paying an unknown person for a service not yet rendered with no possibility of recovering the payment. Online payment services are relatively reasonable in terms of commission and make the funds available to you instantly. They also offer security to the customer, which may encourage participation in the early days. It is worthwhile to set up the mechanism, doing so will also enable you to take credit card payments via the same platform. Though cash may remain king, more and more transactions are electronic now, so embrace it. Again, there are several services available to tutors to streamline payments.

Online lessons are another fantastic way to extend your available working hours - with changes in time zones around the world, you could again find a means to fill otherwise unoccupied time during the working and school days. There are also associated opportunities, the most obvious example being sales of books and other required teaching materials to support the online lesson experience.

Recorded Lessons

Similar to the online lessons previously mentioned, it is also possible to deliver pre-recorded lessons over the internet. Usually on a specific subject, technique or a particular track, pre-recorded lessons served online are becoming increasingly popular via several routes:

★ Personal websites - memberships, subscriptions and pay for access.

★ Video sharing sites, monetised via advertising whilst free to view.

★ Online tuition sites, collating video lessons on a multitude of subjects.

Required equipment will be similar to the previous section: a computer with Internet connection, a video camera, and some editing software unless you're extremely confident in completing the whole video in one-take without any errors. You might want to invest in a better-quality camera for a professional result. These videos could be visible to a significant audience and will become adverts for you, your services and your musicianship, so make sure they're the best you can achieve. Regardless of where you choose to offer your video lessons, make sure you title them professionally, properly credit any parties who were involved in their production, and close with your website address where your prospective customers, students, and fans can find out more.

You will note yet another push for your personal website! If you haven't done so yet, get that domain name registered and start work! You can easily set up a store and accept payments via online payment provider and credit card for downloads of video lessons. Having membership on your site to access video content is helpful for growing a mailing list as well - a number of people who have already expressed an interest in you will likely welcome being contacted with new developments. Another asset for your music business.

Video sharing sites have become ubiquitous in recent years, and you are probably already aware that material on more or less any subject is available. Start your own channel and upload your videos. All the major video sharing platforms allow monetisation of video with the check of a box, so check that box! The key to making money with this approach is traffic; you need people to view your videos, and there are three key methods to maximise that traffic:

★ Use of keywords: the words people search for when looking for your lessons. These could (and should) include your name, or the name you are working under, the topic, and the specific nature of the piece - be it a specific track or technique walkthrough.

★ Linking your video sharing channel pages to your website, and vice-versa.

★ Using social media to encourage your followers to subscribe to your channel and view your videos.

Each view of a video pays pennies, but they build surprisingly quickly. And anything you can do to increase interest in your videos can only magnify that effect.

Finally, there are tuition sites dedicated to more or less any instrument you can think of, and several you have probably never heard of. They tend to have a paid roster of tutors, as well as permitting freelancers to upload content as well. Typically, you will need to sign up to the service in question to take advantage, which could cost £10 / $13 per month as a guide. Once a paying member, you will get access to existing material as well as the right to upload your own. The mechanism for payment is similar to the video sharing sites, you will likely be paid per view. However, these sites have the advantage of an audience that by virtue of their membership have already demonstrated an interest in watching video on your chosen subject. A captive audience, and a pretty close to certain likelihood that your efforts will be well received, provided what you're saying makes sense and your videos are of acceptable quality.

The associated benefit of such sites is that if your video lessons are popular and good quality, you could find yourself being asked to work on staff. This was my experience. Temporarily the overhead increased as I was obliged to create content branded for the site in question, but the amount paid per view increased, as did my profile on the site - which in turn increased views on video sharing sites and to my website.

The big BIG advantage of recorded lessons is the passive income that can be derived from them for years afterwards. Maybe it takes you an hour to plan a video lesson. Then another two hours to produce a five-minute video - that's approximately how long it took me to record, edit and upload each of mine, and write a summary for the page in which the video was displayed. That three-hour investment in time could make you tens of pounds every month for years. As you will see from the real-world examples that close out this section, I continue to make a significant income from video lessons I have not touched at all for over 6 years!

Another income generation strategy that is available to you no matter what your schedule is that you can fit the creation of these video lessons in around the edges of other paying work, doing as much or as little as you wish. When you see for yourself how lucrative they are, you will wish you'd started sooner!

Speciality Lessons

There are many types of lesson available over and above the standard, some I have offered myself and seen others do the same to good effect. Such lessons often attract a premium, but cost no more to provide.

Audition & Recital Prep

These are lessons focussed entirely on a particular event - typically an audition for a band or theatrical performance, a recital, or an entrance examination for a music school. A student will request specific lesson outcomes, and there is almost certainly a time imperative. This type of lesson is typically easier for a tutor in the following respects:

★ Less planning of the lesson, owing to fixed material and defined outcomes.

★ Greater focus from the student, as a result of the incentive driving the lesson.

★ Lower likelihood of 'no-show', with the motivation of the looming event.

Assuming a successful outcome, the lessons can be massively rewarding for both tutor and student. Elements of technique may need to be covered in detail and practiced to perfection, and it may be necessary to work through a specific performance piece in fine detail until the student can perform it flawlessly. I find it pays to be a little harsh in appraisals of performance - not so much that the student is disheartened of course, but a tutor needs to be at least as firm a critic as the final audience will be to maximise the likelihood of a positive outcome. Your students will thank you... one day!

Cover Song Training

Today's video-sharing generation are obsessed with performances of specific pieces for their audience, paying or otherwise. Very few students approach me asking for lessons in sweep picking or two-handed tapping, but plenty as me how to play specific tracks. Perhaps more still ask for simplified versions that still offer the effect of the full track, minus complexity.

Such lessons can attract a premium, especially if you are in a position to provide simplified arrangements for popular pieces. I have had many requests over the years for specific tracks by instrumental guitar players like Joe Satriani and Steve Vai, often from players who are very competent but lack the patience to work through the tracks themselves, or perhaps cannot figure out from notation alone how it is possible to play a particular sequence of notes. All reasonably easily taken care of in a handful of lessons.

There are likely to be 'upsells' available in the form of books, the time taken to compose a simplified version specifically for an individual student and additional lessons to build the techniques necessary to execute certain parts. Speed and dexterity come with practice rather than payment, and there is no alternative to investing time in the endeavour. You might also offer your services to film and edit the completed track. My students seem to enjoy that, and if the piece is reasonably accessible, you might find it is possible to achieve a completed video in an hour session.

Improvisation

Honestly, lessons in improvisation don't even feel like work to me, more an excuse to have a jam with someone and get paid for it! It is a little strange speaking as someone who has an affinity with the improvised elements of playing that others find it hard, but clearly having the chops for it is a big advantage. Back to there being no substitute for time served.

And although that is certainly true, improvement can be accelerated by a good tutor. Clearly, a familiarity with various scales is helpful, as are tips on various stylistic elements a student might wish to employ. Usually when I am approached for lessons in improvisation the student has already reached a good standard and wants to develop their own voice. In these situations, an additional ear to help identify what 'works' musically is the main requirement.

From the point of view of a tutor, you're going to need a firm grasp of keys, scales and modes, as well as good technique. Confidence in yourself is the biggest single 'skill' in improvisation - if you've got some swagger then you're only ever a semi-tone away from a note in key, so provided you can move back or forth like you mean it, you've just added grace notes to the bag of tricks!

Business Management

If you are an experienced musician, getting started in teaching is not hard. Being a good tutor most certainly is, and comes with experience. Far and away the most difficult aspect for a novice tutor is keeping track of your lessons, your students and their progress, exams, who you lent what book to when, and payments.

Finding a system that works is a matter of personal preference, and could be a simple as a paper pad for notes. Spreadsheets on a computer might be the next step along, as well as a calendar. There are also a large number of packaged software solutions available that I've found enormously helpful. There are several out there that will provide you with a website on which students can enrol for lessons, all notes can be kept, payments tracked and processed. A couple even offer integrated video lessons, providing everything you need to run a teaching business.

Usually offered as subscription services, you'll be able to find suitable offerings easily via your favourite search engine. And I recommend doing so. The cost typically amounts to between £10 and £15 per month, which I think is a wise investment considering the amount of time the products can save you.

Potential Income

Established tutors can make £30 per hour; £20 per hour would make you a very persuasive proposition on cost alone but be wary of under-selling yourself or giving the impression of offering an inferior service.

Were we to assume a 35-hour working week and 4 weeks holiday per year, you could be looking at an income of £42,000 per year and an immediate check in the 'success' box. Book over. Done. Mic drop! But if you worked full-time as a music tutor, you'd be a music tutor. Nothing wrong with that, but it might not be what you want. It is technically a career in the music business, but is probably not what you had in mind when you picked up this book.

Teaching is also totally reliant on your time, so will not deliver the freedoms we seek.

Real world example

Teaching full-time was not what I wanted, though I have taught a great deal over the years. When I was starting out I taught a lot more, and people looking for music lessons are never in short supply. One-to-one lessons, online lessons as well as video and screen-presented transcriptions. I now teach a couple of lessons a week with people who I have been teaching for many years and have built friendships with, and I still gather an income of three hundred pounds a month on average from websites that carry my lessons and charge membership subscriptions. I also take a lesson every week, because I feel it is good to be consistently challenged, and to push yourself to achieve more. When I initially made the break from the day job, I was teaching two days a week (15 sessions - £450 per week). Now my teaching income is as below:

One to One Lesson Income (Annual)	£3120
Online Lesson Income (Annual)	£3600
Total	**£6720**
Time Spent (Weekly)	~3hrs

Which means an income from teaching of around **£47 per hour**.

Note that the online lesson income is completely passive. I do not need to do anything at all to receive that income, though I do respond to enquiries from students on the websites by way of continued engagement which only takes a few minutes.

Writing

Overview

★ ★ ★ ☆ ☆   Difficulty

★ ☆ ☆ ☆ ☆   Cost

★ ★ ★ ★ ☆   Time Commitment

★ ★ ★ ☆ ☆   Likelihood of Success

★ ★ ★ ★ ☆   Income Potential

Required resources: available time, an environment free of distractions and a pen and paper, or computer.

Writing isn't hard for most of us, we all do it all the time. If you are in the habit of speaking to people without them falling asleep right in front of you, you have the necessary communication skills within to be a writer. If you are a competent musician as well, no reason you couldn't be writing about music!

Reading is another pastime that has been transformed by technology. Gone are the days of being restricted to physical books, possibly on loan from the local library. We absorb information on our own terms: books, eBooks, Internet articles, various snippets from all manner of sources. Clearly traditional print still very much exists, but information is sought in different forms. It is rare now to sit and read a book in search of one piece of information, when that same information is available in an article or indexed within an eBook. Writers come in all shapes and sizes, and your voice is exactly that, your voice. It will resonate with some, less with others. And so it is with all writers. As above, if you can talk to people without them losing interest or walking away, you could be a writer.

One of the most persuasive arguments in favour of adding writing to your musician's portfolio is the opportunity for passive income. Once you have written something, it has potential to make you money for many months, or even years into the future! There are many avenues open to music writers, and whether you have a lot of time and inclination or not much of either, there is an option that can work for you.

Websites

You're going to need to write content for your own website, but there are thousands of music websites out there, many of which are looking for regular contributors. You may recall from the section on your own website that search engines thrive on new content and sites that are regularly updated.

To keep attracting new readers, websites have an unquenchable thirst for content. There are a large number of people who will provide that content. Known as copywriters - because they write copy (!), there are many individuals who will write articles to customer specs. Some of them live in parts of the world where the cost of living is much lower, and there are always people in the world willing to work for less. There are freelancer sites that connect people who will work for little to those who don't want to pay very much. And they're dealing with the 'filler' content - tons and tons of junk that gets uploaded to keep the search engines entertained, but does very little to engage a human audience. We don't want to compete with that.

This is where a music professional comes in. Someone who actually understands the subject on which he is writing, rather than merely gathering material from the wider Internet and making minor changes to call it their own. Someone who can write an engaging piece that speaks to a like-minded audience. And if you can hold a conversation in a music store, you can write something valuable for a customer.

There are several simple things you can do to secure paying work as a writer for websites. Make sure you list copywriting or freelance writing services on your own website to ensure visitors appreciate that is a skill you possess. Make sure if you are going to market yourself as a writer that your text is accurate in terms of spelling and grammar. You can command a higher rate if your writing is also designed with search engines in mind, and 'ready to go' from the point of view of a website owner. Make sure to have examples of your writing available for viewing on your website. And make sure the pieces you have available are as good as you can make them. Ideally, two or three short pieces of around five hundred words on various subjects, which will provide an introduction to your writing service. One or two longer pieces of a couple of thousand words are also helpful, demonstrating you are able to write a more in-depth piece where appropriate.

You should also contact websites you have found in your own Internet travels, enquiring as to whether they need more contributors. This is an extremely easy approach to make - if you are genuinely a reader of their material as it stands, you are in a position to engage with them on a subject in which you are genuinely interested (and we're back to people liking to work with people they like). Given the choice of engaging someone with a genuine passion for the subject versus someone with a genuine passion for earning money, you don't have to be a genius to figure out which one wins. Widen your horizons by searching out more sites in your preferred musical field, whether they be related to your instrument, music theory, teaching, recording - any subject you have sufficient knowledge of to entertain a conversation on. Even subjects you know little about, but have a genuine interest and appetite to find out more. Approach the sites via their contact pages and ask if they are looking for contributors. You will be surprised how many do. Even from those who don't a flat 'no' is extremely unlikely - you will almost certainly be asked for more information, providing the opportunity to promote your website, and will be offered contact when an opportunity arises. Networking, it is a powerful thing.

What to charge is an interesting question, since we've established there will always be people willing to write for less. My suggestion is you establish a value for your time and quote based on the time it takes to create a piece. You might want to consider the other paying alternatives for your time, and with that in mind we could work on the assumption an hour spent writing could have made you £30 / $40 if teaching. On that basis, a 500-word article might take you an hour to produce and £30 would be a fair price to charge. The more experienced you are as a writer, the higher your prices can defensibly be. If you are in demand you can name your price, at least until you get to the point that customers start to tail off.

Make sure you include any time you will spend researching the subject when you are quoting for work. A 500-word article, well written and researched, with text structured appropriately for its purpose could make you £100 from the right audience and £50 very easily indeed. That article could have been written in an hour, making writing for websites very lucrative indeed, and certainly worth including in your portfolio of services

Blogs

Pretty much a modern-day diary, we have already discussed the use of blogs on your own website to ensure regular updates. New material on websites encourages search engines to rank them higher, which encourages more people to visit, which encourages the site owner to develop more content… and around and around we go.

You can make money from blogs just as you would make money from your own website more generally, by adding advertising and being paid by the mouse click. It will not pull in a fortune unless you get really serious traffic volumes, but it is another one of those things that takes seconds to set up and can make you a few pounds/dollars here and there, which contribute to your greater goal of success for zero effort going forward. And that is exactly the kind of income we're looking for!

There are several organisations in the paid online advertising market, most of them being the major players in the search engine market. Businesses pay the search companies to advertise their services, and the search providers as a result need sites willing to display those ads. The search engines take the advertising money, pay an amount of it to those willing to host the ads, and keep the difference between the two. To make money from advertising on your website, you will need people to visit your site, and ideally to click on the adverts themselves. You will get a few pennies for each visitor to your site (a view of an advert is called an impression) and a few more pennies should a site visitor click on the advert. If you get to the point of generating thousands of visitors per day, you can make tens of pounds from advertising each day, which soon mounts up to a decent annual figure.

You may need to meet certain qualifying criteria for the advertising companies, specifically you will need the home, about and contact pages we have discussed previously. You will also need a privacy page that talks about how your site uses the viewer's personal information. This is because the advertisers use little snippets of code, called cookies, to note what sort of topics a person searches for, and use that data to display relevant ads to them. Once you have those pages, and an amount of content a viewer would find engaging, apply for the advertising programs. Once accepted, you will be provided with the code to add to your website, and instructions with which to complete the necessary steps. It literally takes a few minutes, and as I have explained, could make you money every day afterwards for literally no effort at all.

It may take a few moments every few days to keep your blog current. This is an activity that pays dividends regardless of advertising revenue. As a professional musician, you need your audience to know where you are playing, what you are doing, where they can hear more from you and so on. Having all the updates in one place is a fantastic strategy and you can link to it from anywhere and everywhere. Make sure you configure your blog to automatically post to social media - that way you get multiple benefits from a single piece of content, and ensure it is received by as wide an audience as possible.

It is also possible to secure a spot on other people's blogs. As per the previous section, the majority of websites want traffic, and traffic comes to those who update - so bloggers need content too. Payment can come in several forms:

★ Find reciprocal arrangements with other people, and take advantage of their writing skills to create additional content for your site, while you create for theirs.

★ Include your name and a link back to your own site, widening your audience.

★ Negotiate a percentage of advertising revenue from pages displaying your content.

★ Actually get paid, in the manner described in the previous section. £50 for a quality 500-word article is completely achievable.

Perhaps even elements of all the above. Blogging is a field where there are no rules and no entry criteria, you can develop your own voice and become authoritative in your field. This can also feed into the establishment of a brand, as your name becomes more and more widely known. Make sure you always get credit as an author and a link back to your site. Some content providers want to appear the source of all content on their sites; in this event, you should charge more for the written work to offset the loss of exposure and potential traffic back to you.

Digital Magazines & Newsletters

Traditional print media can be a little inaccessible to those without relevant qualifications and experiences in the field, or those yet to make a name for themselves. But fear not! It is possible to be a successful contributor to digital publications with no such background. Using articles on your website, blog and any copy you can reference as your existing body of work, you will be adequately qualified for work writing articles for digital publications.

Starting out in this field is likely to mean fitting in with the editorial style of the wider publication, it is unlikely that an editor will want you to approach the job too idiosyncratically in the first instance, especially if you are not yet a recognised name. As you become more established, it may become appropriate to be more individual stylistically. Some of my first paid writing jobs were a series of articles on music theory, from the most basic beginnings to some fairly advanced material over the course of many months. They started reasonably dry and factual but, as I developed a familiar structure, I found myself able to be a little looser with language. I eventually become pretty unique in my writing style, even managing to work in an occasional joke! I was only granted the freedom to indulge my creative excesses once I had established a foundation of value. Once it was clear the readership were interested in what I had to say, I was more able to experiment with how I said it.

Securing this kind of work is similar to writing articles for websites. You will get the best results by approaching publications you already have familiarity with, all of whom are forever in need of content. In this instance because they are charging their subscribers a fee for a product, and that product needs to be of appropriate quality. Seek out contact details from company web pages; you may also find an email address for an editor in the publications themselves. Provided you have a portfolio of work to reference and your email is short and to the point, communicating a genuine interest, you can expect a favourable response.

Income from digital publications is variable, and based primarily on their circulation figures. A 'bottom line' income should be in line with writing articles for websites and blogs, but since the word count requirement is likely to triple, you can expect the payment to do so as well. £200 for a 1,500-word article is realistic, and such an article could amount to 3 hours of work assuming modest research and fact checking is required. I was paid several hundred pounds per month for many years by a subscription-driven guitar website boasting 2 million members. I provided articles for a newsletter and edited the whole thing together, which took a couple of hours per month.

Copywriting and Content Services

There are several companies out there who will tell you they can get you writing work immediately, no problem. Register, give them a list of the subjects on which you are happy to write, and away you go. Some of them will give you an assessment piece to complete within a specific timeframe, whilst others just accept your application and offer you access to a marketplace where writing jobs are offered. Those writing jobs are usually pretty simple, pretty vague, and with pretty low word counts, making them quick and easy to do. Sounds great right? There is always a but…

Actually, it's almost all 'buts'. The first, and most notable is 'but they keep most of the money'. I have no idea how much they charge companies for their copy service, but I can tell you they pay literally pennies per word. You would have to write a spectacular amount to make it pay well. The second 'but' will be 'but you don't get any credit for the writing' - you will not be able to add your name or website address to any writing you sell this way, meaning no opportunity to make additional income from it. You will very likely not even know when or where your writing has been published. Hot on the heels of that comes "but you won't get any ongoing payment from royalties", as effectively an employee of the company, your writing becomes their property at the point they pay you. Overall, not at all satisfactory.

If you really REALLY need the money, I guess it is OK in a pinch. The writing company will pay you the amount agreed ahead of time pretty much immediately, so if you are in need of money fast it could be an option. But those I have seen seriously under-value the contributions of their writers and I would assume attract writers from places where the cost of living is much reduced, and a couple of pounds much more attractive a proposition. They, in my judgement, distort the market and undermine skilled copy and content writers by encouraging a race to the bottom driven by ever-reducing costs.

They may or may not offer a bargain service to their customers, but I suspect they are simply making good money by playing the middleman to paying clients and cut-price 'writers'. Charging one a competitive but significant price, whilst paying the other a fraction of it. In short, you can do much much better.

I would encourage you to sell your writing services directly from your website and by approaching potential customers directly, referencing your portfolio of work. Use a copywriting service to get work if you absolutely must, but I would not advise getting into the habit of it. You are unlikely to receive even 10% of what you would have if writing directly for a client. I would certainly never advocate you engage such a company to provide content for your site. It will not be up to the level of quality you expect, and will not reflect well of you or your brand.

Books

Until a decade or so ago, getting a book published was a pretty arduous process. Sending manuscripts to agents and publishers, and probably getting rejections from all and sundry. Even very successful authors often tell the tales of their multiple rejections before finally breaking through. Being an author was not for everyone, and could easily amount to a full-time job in its own right.

The Internet has revolutionised the book market, not least with the advent of the eBook and eReader. Books are now downloadable onto mobile devices and may only exist in electronic form, many books today not even making it to paperback. The tools and systems that make electronic books possible also permit cheap and on-demand printing, reducing cost and making printing books accessible to everyone. And suddenly everyone can be a writer. It is said everyone has a book in them just waiting to come out, and there is no reason you should be any different. If it takes around an hour to write 1,000 words, a typical eBook at 20,000 words could be produced in 20 hours, probably meaning it could be created in a couple of weeks comfortably using free time arranged around paid work. A full paperback, typically 80 - 120,000 words, would, of course take longer to put together, but could conceivably be written in a month. Again, with writing sessions structured around paid work and other commitments.

Subject Matter

What would you write a book about? Writing about what you know is a fantastic place to start. Obviously, I've written this book on being successful in the music business without being a star, having found myself being successful in the music business, without being a star! I hope others will find value in the approaches I used myself to build an income from what used to be a hobby. Regardless, I am drawing on my experiences of paying my bills with music for well over a decade, to help others understand how they could do the same.

For a musician, one's primary instrument is often extremely fertile ground. If you have become proficient enough to consider making music your living, you are very likely to possess insights that others would appreciate. If you have started teaching, perhaps yet more still. If you've toured, played gigs to which nobody turned up, played a sold-out stadium show... you have stories to tell. One of my first solo performances saw me playing first on the bill at a blues show. My curtain call came, and I tried to stall since I could see for myself there was nobody there. The proprietor of the establishment wanted some music to help pull people in from outside, so I was obliged to start. I must have played to the bar staff for the first 15 minutes before people slowly drifted in. By the end I'd drawn quite a crowd, and it turned out pretty well from the point of view of an ongoing residency for a couple of years... but that was a very very slow start. There is probably a book of rock and roll horror stories in me yet! And there is likely a book in you too.

If you as a musician are interested in what you do, there is every possibility and likelihood that other musicians will be interested in what you have to say about it. Maybe you're a seasoned producer with tips to share. Perhaps you're an absolute genius of a session musician, with advice to share on versatility and building chops. Perhaps you are a heroic drunkard, familiar with playing whilst whisky-blind. Whatever it is, consider writing a book about it. The process will definitely help you to become a better writer, to develop your unique voice as a writer, as well as building a reputation and extending your brand. Becoming authoritative on a subject can easily lead to more work in future, and the entire book can serve as a portfolio of your work for potential clients.

You will end up with a product to sell on your website, as well as being listed by online and high street bookstores - all of which helps to get your name out there and maintain your profile as a musician.

Getting Published

Let's assume you've now written a book and you're ready to release it to your adoring public. Right now you have a word processed document, checked for spelling, and hopefully proofread by a few trusted friends or family members.

Up until around 10 years or so ago your options for self-publishing were pretty limited. There were a few small publishers willing to complete small print runs for a few thousand pounds/dollars or [insert your local currency here]. You could set yourself up as a publisher - technically self-publishing, but a TON of work. Or, you could print yourself and do as best you could.

There have been several improvements over the years, print on demand, or POD, being key amongst them. But everything really changed in 2007. The eBook revolutionised the industry and created new routes to market for experienced and novice authors alike. Today, most self-publishing authors get the majority of their sales in the eBook format. Most book sales today happen through Amazon, which doesn't surprise anyone. Thanks to Amazon tools, hundreds of thousands of authors are publishing their works right now. They are doing everything themselves from typesetting and printing on demand, to organising distribution and marketing. It is possible for today's authors to turn a PDF copy of their new book into to a paid eBook available for customers to download in less time than it takes to drink a cup of coffee.

The easiest option for a novice self-publisher is Amazon's CreateSpace. It may remain the best option for the experienced author as well. Register and set up your book with Ingram Spark at the same time. They require the same information as Amazon to get print on demand set up and their costs are broadly similar, but Ingram have one key advantage. They will list your book in catalogues for real bookshops to order as necessary, this will also mean that the bookstores list your book on their websites as available for order - and it is having your book listed in real stores that, to me, makes your book a real, published book.

You will need an ISBN number. You'll actually need one for each version of your book - hardcover, paperback, and eBook. Some self-publishing services will provide ISBN numbers for you, but as they are assigned to publishing houses this will likely have an impact on the listed publisher of your book, which may not suit you. CreateSpace provided ISBN numbers endow books bearing them with a 'published by CreateSpace' moniker. This has no impact on your rights as an author, but may not be your desired result for your book.

I recommend purchasing your own ISBN numbers. In the UK Nielsen is the issuing authority. You will need to register as a publisher and pay for the number of ISBNs you require. Nielsen also maintain a register of books against ISBN numbers, providing more exposure for you and your new book. The process can be a little ponderous, with forms to fill in that are checked by humans. It is worthwhile getting the ISBN registration and number request started as soon as possible to avoid unnecessary delays with the remainder of the process to get your book published.

For Print on Demand setup both Amazon and Ingram require you to register as a publisher, unless you are taking advantage of one of their self-publishing services. They can take care of pretty much everything for you, but if you take the option you will not have as much control. It will also cost you more. Amazon offer a number of services for editing, layout, cover design, eBook conversion, and marketing.

You will need the following information to set up for printing via CreateSpace:

★ Title

★ Author Name

★ Language

★ ISBN Number

★ Your print-ready book PDF

★ Book Dimensions (page size and count)

★ Cover image and finish choice

You are then required to approve and accept a digital proof. You will be prompted if any text extends beyond the printable area. You will need to correct this or risk cutting off text. You will also be prompted if any images included in the print are of insufficient quality (all images must be 300dpi minimum). Once you have approved your digital proof, your book is ready to list via the various distribution channels and is prepared for sale.

I would heartily recommend ordering a copy for direct delivery first, just to check the quality of the print and to ensure everything is as it should be. My first CreateSpace book looked great in digital proof, but the physical copy saw every bullet point replaced with a '[?]' akin to an HTML image load failure. Not ideal, and easily remedied with a different bullet. It would have made for a poor experience for the reader had I not checked a physical book. So please check a physical copy. This is your reputation as an author we're talking about here.

Ingram's requirements are broadly similar to Amazon's so I won't repeat the information previously offered, but there is one key point to note. Their rendering of a digital file can differ from CreateSpace's. Please do not simply upload the same PDF to Ingram as you've just approved with CreateSpace and assume everything will be fine. Make sure to check the digital proof carefully as well as reviewing a physical copy before approving the final version.

In terms of distribution, Amazon will be your primary route to market. It will come as no surprise that many of the distribution options offered by their platform are Amazon-centric. Assuming your book is printed in English, selecting Amazon.com and Amazon Europe for distribution is a bit of a no-brainer.

If you used a CreateSpace issued ISBN, you can select the 'Bookstores and Online Retailers' distribution option. Similarly, if you are printing an academic text and used a CreateSpace issued ISBN, you would be eligible for the 'Libraries and Academic Institutions' distribution option.

To get your book into bookstores, or at least onto their websites and in their order books, you need Ingram. The process is similar to Amazon. As soon as you are registered as a publisher and have approved a digital proof, you can mark your book for distribution. This will result in your title and all listed details being circulated to bookstores throughout the country.

Ingram will notify you when an organisation in receipt of their catalogue requests copies of your book. You will then need to initiate the print on demand process to fulfil the order. Simple.

Finally, a note on taxes: Amazon as a US-Company is legally obliged to withhold 30% of royalties on your sales via Amazon.com to pass on to the IRS. You could argue that if you're not selling much via '.com' then 30% of not much isn't enough to worry about. I believe that your income is your income. Completing a form to state you are not a US citizen, although seemingly rather odd, is easy enough to do. On a related theme, I have had to make a similar declaration to the authorities in Singapore to retain all my royalty income. Again, no major hardship and all those pounds soon add up.

There are references all over the Internet to people calling the IRS and other national tax authorities, making it seem daunting. I have never had to speak to anybody, merely complete online forms and click 'Submit'. I recommend you do the same.

Sheet Music Transcription

You are no doubt aware that sales of notation can bring in a sizeable income for an artist - you need only observe in your local bookshop the fact that a book containing the score of an album costs more than the CD to know this to be true. You may be surprised to hear that many (many) artists performing today have no formal music education, and cannot read or write a note. And between those two constituent facts, lies yet another opportunity for a working musician.

If you are a capable reader of music, comfortable with theory, you already have the majority of the tools required for transcription services. Skills in notation are clearly a requirement, as is the ability to listen to a song and write it out. Learning by ear is second nature to most musicians, and the recording is very likely to be your source material. If you are confident about that concept, this can be a solid source of income.

Assuming you have the skills required to perform the task, getting work in transcription is pretty simple, particularly as musicians who can read and write notation are a minority set against those performing it. List the service on your website, and let it be known via social media that transcription is a service you provide. The majority of labels have an in-house provision for transcription, but independents are potential customers. The going rate to transcribe a song can range from £60 - £200, depending on the customer as well and the length and complexity of the piece. Even simple proofreading of a score will pay up to £50.

Guitarists are notoriously unlikely readers of music, so seeking out Internet forums and social media groups where they congregate may produce rapid success. Classical musicians, conversely, are far more likely to participate fully with notation, and are likely to have less of a need for such a service.

Any busy musician however, regardless of competence, may prefer to outsource their transcription work simply to avoid the effort. It can take a couple of hours to transcribe a track, less with a practiced ear, but even at a couple of hours of work music transcription can deliver a compelling hourly rate, perhaps up to £100 per hour. Proofreading notation can also be tremendously lucrative, and may only take minutes for a score. The amount of time taken is heavily dependent on the quality of source material; a good score requiring minimal intervention could amount to money for nothing, where a disaster of a piece could require enormous effort, potentially not being worth the time. Experience has to be your guide here; you are likely to acquire repeat custom, and you will know from previous dealings how much time and effort is likely to be required. I would recommend an hourly fee with an agreed duration, revisited if a score needs substantially more work than first envisioned.

If you can read music competently, I would strongly suggest offering a transcription service on your website. Even if uptake is limited, it strengthens your offering as a music professional. It also showcases your versatility, demonstrating your usefulness to as many people as possible and maximising your income potential, as well as providing another networking opportunity; today's job could be transcription but tomorrow's could be something more exciting or lucrative!

Writing for free

I do not typically advocate working for free, or for 'exposure' as the popular phrase suggests when it comes to performance. If you are writing in time that would otherwise not be used productively, you take your choices I guess, but it is a poor decision to undertake pro bono work when you could be being paid. My more specific rule of thumb is never to work for free if the person you are working for will be paid - I have no problem with charity stuff, and I do volunteer work every month, but not for a guy who makes money from it. I have heard it expressed as follows:

> *"In order for someone to get something*
> *for nothing, someone else must be getting*
> *nothing for something."*

And that doesn't sound very fair, does it?

It might be that you can see circumstances where writing for a particular organisation at no charge could increase your circulation, bringing you to new audiences you would otherwise not have access to. If this is your desire, make sure the practices of the organisation in question allow you to name yourself as the author and link back to your main page. If writing is being provided at no fee, I would also expect to retain full rights to the work, and be able to publish it as I saw fit - no exclusivity for no payment. Maybe you feel that after a couple of pieces provided at no cost to prove your talent, you will be paid subsequently. There is a place for 'nothing ventured, nothing gained', but seek to satisfy yourself that this will indeed come to pass. With so many content providers and aggregators out there, finding a paying one is not difficult.

Many websites will tell you they will 'showcase' your written work, some even charge you for the privilege, but all are looking to make an income from your work one way or another. Do not be fooled - you can make a perfectly good income representing yourself.

From finding places that pay to suggestions on style and content if you're getting knockbacks but no feedback; If you really struggle to find paid writing work contact me via mmimusicbooks.com and I'll point you in the right direction, no charge, no trouble.

Potential Income

Writing a 500-word article can be easily achieved in one hour, assuming the article is on a subject known reasonably well, and research is more in the realm of fact-checking. Once you are more practiced, 1,000-word is more than possible within an hour. That article could sell for between £50 and £100 at minimum, as well as providing content for your website and blog, driving traffic and increasing advertising revenue there. Taking a conservative £75 median figure for an article, assuming a 35-hour working week and 4 weeks' holiday per year, you could be looking at an income of £126,000 per year! I would consider that stupendous, never mind successful! Imagine a six-figure income, working from home and with hours that suited you! I feel like we're making progress toward the freedom dream here. But if you worked full-time as a music writer, you'd be a music writer. No shame in that at all, but it might not be what you want. It is absolutely a career in the music business, but is probably not what you had in mind when you picked up this book. The good news though is that all your written work can keep on paying you in future - a passive income not reliant on your time, though the rewards gathered are completely proportional to the amount you put in.

If we assume you can write around 1,000-words per hour, and take the following figures for modestly successful texts selling on your favourite Internet bookstore:

★ A typical eBook is 20,000 words long and makes £150 per month.

★ A typical non-fiction book is 50,000 words long and makes £250 per month.

Making the income per hour of effort £90 for an eBook and £60 for a book based on the indicative figures given. Not bad for an hourly rate. The real triumph comes later - that with no effort whatsoever that eBook will make you £1800 next year and the paperback will make you £3,000. And again the year after, and the year after. More of that glorious passive income that hopefully you're beginning to see can transform your working life. It will also make you a bona fide author, with a book to sell on your website and perhaps a better profile as a writer, which will help when seeking writing work elsewhere. Writing a book cannot fail to make you a better writer!

Real world example

Writing full-time has never been an aspiration of mine, though I do write daily for my various websites, as well as providing articles for a tuition website and curating the content of another. I have mentioned previously earning around £1000 a month from a single site, writing articles and editing others. It is also completely realistic to find ten sites requiring ten articles per month at £100 each - and suddenly there's that six-figure income again! It might only take you 20 hours per week to achieve it as well.

I have written several books, all of which are available as paperbacks and eBooks from online and real-world retailers. You are reading one of them now! You will hopefully appreciate that I do not know yet how well this book will sell. I hope it either already is, or very soon will, give you the tools and insights to make music your livelihood. The figure below for book sales is based only on my first book.

eBook & Paperback Sales (Annual)	£3000
Website Articles (Annual)	£4800
Total	**£7800**
Time Spent (Monthly)	~3hrs

The book took me approximately 20 hours to write and set up for sale three years ago, but has not taken a second of my time ever since. £3000 per year, for absolutely zero effort! The 3 hours per month is spent writing articles for websites with whom I have established relationships, and I can fit in that time whenever convenient. Making use of time that would otherwise not be used.

Whatever you write, make sure you make it work as hard as possible for you. Re-publishing works in full, serialised, or as excerpts on your own site, can drive more writing business as well as keeping your website current with traffic heading toward it. More content means more advertising revenue, more site visitors and higher search rankings. More content will also build an ever-increasingly persuasive portfolio for prospective clients, improving the chances of success exponentially. If you are a capable musician, able to communicate effectively with an audience, you will make a fine writer. All it takes is practice!

Performance

Overview

★ ★ ★ ★ ★   Difficulty

★ ★ ★ ☆ ☆   Cost

★ ★ ☆ ☆ ☆   Time Commitment

★ ★ ★ ☆ ☆   Likelihood of Success

★ ★ ★ ★ ☆   Income Potential

Required resources - Instruments and PA equipment, a group of like-minded people (if appropriate) and a paying audience!

Performance is a staple for a musician - most of us started playing because we saw someone doing something amazing with a guitar, piano or whatever. It can be a good revenue stream as well, with income from recorded music eroded by the various digital services.

Live performance is the original way to make a living from making music. Long before the recorded music industry ever existed, musicians were out there performing to paying audiences. While revenue has dropped massively for record labels, live shows continue to do well. Experience is king today; a live performance can be recorded, but it cannot be duplicated. You have to be in the crowd to experience it. Music is an accompaniment to our daily lives. Think about how often you hear silence today - not often is it? There is live music everywhere, from the archetypal shows in bars and halls on the weekends to cafes, libraries and colleges. People want live music at their events, whether big or small, and all that music has to be performed by somebody. And that somebody could be you!

Once again, the Internet has revolutionised the performance world. Gone are the days of handing flyers out to the audience mid-gig (though in fairness it still works really well!), you now have a global audience at your fingertips every minute of every day. Getting the word out for your up-coming performance via your own website and social media can be done with a handful of mouse clicks. Listing your availability for functions, shows and intimate house shows has never been easier. Recording your shows for new audio releases and monetised video is easy, and the revenue streams ongoing. Overall, if you're not performing as a professional musician you are missing out on the most authentic of musical experiences, but more importantly, right now you're missing out on a solid chunk of income!

The single biggest piece of advice I can give anyone aspiring to more performance work is to be likeable. Make an effort for people, make them feel you care about their show and give them confidence you will do a fantastic job for them. The people talking to you about live work desperately want you to be awesome, so have a show reel that demonstrates how awesome you are, and help them understand you're a good choice. People like working with people they like, and prefer paying people they like as well.

Gigs

It is pretty likely you're already aware of the possibility of making money from live shows. Pubs, clubs, bars and purpose-built venues have music performances every night of the week. The headline acts need support; large venues often have additional performers in waiting areas or start the program even earlier with additional acts. We're not going to spend much time talking about building a profile and sending out demo tapes, mostly because 1) you should have already read the section on the importance or profile, as well as seeing repeated prompts to create a website and 2) Demo Tapes? Really? Since the Internet came along we're kind of past that!

Assuming you have got your website together, you will want a section devoted to your live performance, as well as your band if you're working as a group. Sound clips, songs and video should be a part of this, meaning that any approach to the management of a venue can be covered with a conversation and a card with your website address printed on it, or an email with all the information required for a booking, and details for the website. Now approaches for paid performance take seconds, and once all your website material is together you can give anyone and everyone a very good idea of what you're about quickly and easily.

For the purposes of this section, we'll assume you and your gang can play well enough to get a gig. And I know you can; if you're not quite 'there' yet, practice. One of you must have a garage or some understanding housemates. You will get better, and honestly there is no faster way to get better than to suck Live. You will never want to repeat that experience, trust me! As you get better, you will draw the eye of bigger venues with better line ups, who pay more. You are very likely to start small and be paid in beer or a door percentage. If you can project a professional look from your website and throughout your dealings with venue proprietors, insist on being paid upfront as one business providing services to another business. Although door receipts and ticket sales are great, keep in mind that venues of all sizes typically make more money from selling drinks and food to the paying public as they do from ticket sales.

Also, keep in mind that the gig is in effect your opportunity to appear at the sales event, the people in attendance are your customers, and there are plenty of other ways to get paid at a gig besides the ticket sales or flat fee!

If you've got a CD on sale, take some copies to the venue and make sure everybody knows you have a CD available. People paying for a show will typically buy into the act they are watching, and be willing to invest if they like what they hear. A great way to increase sales is to mention a CD during a break between songs, then take a walk around the crowd after your show. Not while another band is playing, that would be disrespectful, but during the transition between acts go meet and greet your paying public! A full on 'merch' stand at a small show might not be appropriate, but having someone crowd-side with a few shirts, CDs, postcards with your website details on and so on will make you additional income, as well as converting a few casual people who came on a whim, or happened to be in the bar when you started playing, into fans of the future. I have always made far more money from sales of CDs and shirts than I ever did from ticket sales. If you want to maximise sales, think of the best 'people' person you know. Ask them to come to your show and make sure to ask every person who walks by if they want to buy a CD, paying them a commission based on those sales. You can't lose!

You should also consider recording the show. It is really easy to record a live performance since the house PA system is already pumping your sound from the stage to the room. Record from the mixing desk and you're 90% of the way to a Live album for very little additional effort, and zero studio fees. Video the performance and you have the potential for a Live DVD, downloads from your website (paid or free for promotional purposes), as well as uploading individual tracks to video sharing sites and monetising via advertising. All these routes for additional income from one show. Maybe not every show for the Live CDs and DVDs, but the more video you get onto the Internet with advertising, the quicker that income will become significant.

Don't forget about royalties! When performing your own original material, you can earn royalties from live performances. Regardless of venue, Performance Rights Organizations (PROs) will pay royalties from those live performances. If you haven't signed up with a royalty collection company, find out who collects royalties in your country and get registered. A simple Internet search will answer your question, in the UK royalties are collected by the Performing Right Society (PRS) whilst in the US it is Broadcast Music Inc. (BMI). Not signing up with the royalty collection companies is a big mistake - you're leaving your money on the table. The royalty companies collect up all the money and distribute it amongst the performing artists. It won't be a fortune, but every little bit helps!

Weddings, Funerals and Bar Mitzvahs

Another popular route to a paid performance, providing music for a function is a solid payday. Generally a great deal more lucrative than a gig based on the same level of attendance, and because they're typically organised by individuals with an intimate interest in a positive outcome you can be very confident of getting paid, usually in advance.

You may have seen the film 'The Wedding Singer', in which Adam Sandler's character works through nightmare show after nightmare show, has a bit of a breakdown and is in general depicted as a lovable loser. This being Hollywood, he is saved by the love of a good woman, who presents him with some personalised manuscript paper and an instruction to follow his dreams - be a star! I quite enjoyed the film but its core premise didn't really land with me; that a musician playing such functions is a loser. The film would not have worked particularly well if they'd explained how much money you can get paid, particularly for playing a wedding! Seriously, if you could do it full-time you'd be very very comfortable indeed. £500 for two hours' work is pretty good, right? Well, top class function venues are hosting reception events where the talent is being paid exactly that tonight.

As ever, your website should include all the services you provide, and if playing functions is one of them, list it. Include video of you performing at a similar function, or at least working through some excerpts of your repertoire to allow potential bookings to see you in action. It is important here that you include video of you, and your band if appropriate, dressed for a formal function. The angry rock band look is fine in its place, but someone looking to book some musical performance for a function does not want ripped jeans and tattoos - at least not until after hours! Shirts and ties, looking reasonably clean and tidy will get you significantly more bookings.

List your full repertoire as well - if you don't know classic wedding songs and a few classical pieces, learn them. Once they are part of your repertoire, make sure they're on your website and available on video. After that, it is helpful to have a broad repertoire in several styles and spanning several decades, since your audience is likely to include people from 8 to 80, probably beyond. I've heard a rock band performing the themes from children's TV shows, and I've heard a string quartet playing Metallica, both of which worked really well, were entertaining at the time, and stuck in the mind long afterwards. Listing your repertoire provides a potential customer with as much information as possible about your offering, as well as the opportunity to give you ten songs, as a for instance, that they'd like to hear on the day.

There is, of course, less of an opportunity in such circumstances for 'upselling' - it would not be appropriate to wander around a ceremony, or a social gathering related to it, with an arm full of CDs and flyers. Nothing wrong with having a few CDs propped up somewhere near you, and some cards printed so anyone watching you can make a booking enquiry in future. Class is important there though, and you have to let them come to you, no matter how strong the temptation.

In addition to your website, there are several companies online who maintain directories of function bands, usually organised by geographical area. If you are looking for work in this sector, it may be worthwhile paying for a listing. The cost is usually nominal when set against the potential income, and offers another opportunity to link to your website and drive more traffic. More traffic to your website means more advertising revenue, and getting your videos viewed on the various platforms means more income there. In short, a well-placed listing and positive response can result in the increased traffic paying the listing fee. Some of the sites work a simple 'cost per performance' approach, where you provide a summary of services and a cost per hour, whilst others allow potential customers to list their requirements and you can respond with a proposal and indicative fee. The latter allows for flexibility and engagement with the paying customer, so is probably preferable, but does require more of an investment in time.

It also pays to get to know local venues. When someone books a hotel for a wedding reception or similar function, guess what they start asking next? Recommendations for all the other services they need of course! If they want a band and the venue is in a position to provide details of groups they can recommend, that could be an absolute gift for you. Back to being likeable again. Approach venues with CDs, details of your website and links for videos showing performances in formal settings - preferably an eclectic selection showcasing your versatility and talent. If they like you and consider your work to be of an acceptable standard, why wouldn't they recommend you? After getting over that initial bump they'll be able to recommend you in the future from direct experience. If their customer is happy, so are they.

I can appreciate that many musicians hate the idea of being a covers artist, but consider the fact that you probably already have a good repertoire under your fingers, and let's assume you own at least one smart set of clothes... you're already set up and ready to go. Not to mention the fact that a couple of performances a week could see you achieve the 'success' line of covering our arbitrary £30K / $40K salary, giving you the rest of the week off to work on your own material. There is nothing to stop you setting up a second band name for this kind of work if you're concerned about compromising your artistic integrity. There is also nothing to stop you putting your own stamp on your cover material, thereby making it your own. There is no shame in that at all. List the service on your website, and worry about your credibility as an artist when somebody approaches you for a gig!

Dep

Deputising for a regular band member, or 'Dep', can be a pretty exciting way to get paid for a performance. Every band will, at some point, need to temporarily replace a member who is ill, injured, delayed by some sort of implausible chain of events, or got a better offer and let everyone down. And once again, an opportunity means a payday.

It is easy to overlook the fact that a musician willing to deputise will likely need to be more accomplished than the individual he is replacing. The regular band member has the advantage of rehearsals and possibly several nights recently playing through exactly the same material with the same group. It is very likely that the Dep will have had very little notice, and if they're lucky a set list and some chords. It can be a really crazy ride. You might get a call one day to join a jazz fusion band, which could work out fine since no matter how avant-garde you get, it's unlikely you will be the maddest hatter on the stage. Your next call could be to chugga-chugga barre chords with a pop-punk outfit, which will be a less daunting proposition technically, but could again provide a challenge as an unfamiliar genre.

The principal advantages to Dep work are the variety and the money; by definition events leading to a last minute need to replace a band member are unexpected, and the performance is scheduled. The band need someone to fill the shoes of the missing individual to provide a full show for a paying audience, and they need them in a hurry. If you are a capable and confident musician, you could expect to be paid roughly twice the going rate as part of the group. A couple of hundred pounds for an hour and a half or so is realistic. The band hiring you should expect to simplify the arrangement a touch to account for the fact the Dep will not be as familiar with the piece, which is where key and chord chart come in. From the point of view of someone new to the concept, fitting in with the wider group is job number one. You are not being paid to stand out; you are expected to play the part and fill the musical function of the missing individual. In that instance, less is often more. Better to strum a chord in a rhythm that makes sense than play an elaborate fill that cuts across everybody else.

The principal disadvantage obviously is that Dep work just 'happens', or doesn't. It would be impossible to build a career solely on deputising for other players since you can't possibly know how much demand there will be for your services. You can improve your odds again by being in touch with local venues. If a guitarist is going to fall down a run of stairs and injure his hand, you want it to be your number that gets the call in that moment of crisis. The increase in hourly income will be partially offset by the inability to sell additional products - if you're at a venue as the drummer for a band, it would be pretty bad form to be pushing your own CDs or handing out cards. You're an employee in this context, and as far as the audience is concerned, a full-time member of the band.

By all means, as always, list the service on your website. As you secure Dep work, be sure to include the specifics of past engagements to demonstrate your abilities. Additionally, many websites exist where musicians can list themselves as available for Dep. Some charge for the privilege, whilst others are driven by advertising. Make sure you include a mobile number in any listing - time may well not permit an in-depth browse of suitable candidates. Although not very flattering, you may find yourself getting a job by virtue of being the only trumpet player who could get to the venue inside an hour, and who answered the phone!

Busking

Wow, have I had some fun busking. The ability to work at the literal drop of a hat is somewhat reliant on your chosen instrument. It would be tricky to get a baby grand piano down the subway steps, but provided you have a vaguely portable option available, busking could well be a nice earner for you.

Busking is an opportunity to make an easy £30 in an hour if you're in a busy location. If you're good, people will offer a few coins. If you're not quite so good, a surprising number of people will appreciate that it takes courage to give it a go and will happily reward you. I've yet to see anyone genuinely terrible being offered £20 to stop playing and go away, but I guess you never know! As always have a few CDs available for sale, propped up in your guitar case, along with some cards or flyers. Printed material should be well produced, with an address for your website and social media pages prominently displayed. If you are promoting your work as a band with an upcoming gig, make sure you have means to let people know where they can hear more of you. If you also perform in a function band, a small and well-produced sign detailing your services is also worthwhile, and that sign could jut be a laminated sheet of A4 - it doesn't need to be anything over the top.

Busy retail locations around lunchtime are generally a good bet. Position yourself on a route well travelled to maximise the number of people happening by. Make sure you have appropriate permits to busk in your chosen location - you don't need to be making a sharp exit with a load of gear in tow, and you still have a reputation to maintain. You wouldn't want to be out in the world representing your business and for people to see you being 'moved on'.

Busking is, for me at least, a situational and transitory thing. I used to sit in Manchester station playing my guitar until I had the money for my journey. And it worked pretty well, never taking more than an hour to achieve that objective. It is also a great way to overcome any difficulties with playing in front of people since you get all kinds of reactions, but even the negative ones can be re-framed very easily. The guy who walked briskly past you, barely taking any notice and certainly not offering you any money, was probably in a hurry rather than thinking how terrible you were.

Busking is another enterprise in which you will be massively more successful if you can build a rapport with people. Look like you're enjoying it, smile and make eye contact - not creepy eye contact, just look around and make sure you engage with passers-by. When someone does give you some money, thank them. If you're in full flight, a nod, a thumbs up or a cheeky wink all work. Saying 'thank you' is doubly good, because it lets everyone else in earshot know that someone just gave you money, which will encourage them to do the same.

Performing for free

I do not typically advocate working for free, or for 'exposure' as the popular phrase suggests. If you are willing to take a chance with a new venue, you take your choices, but it is not a good habit to get in to. My more specific rule of thumb is never to work for free if the person you are working for will be paid. I have no problem with charity work, and I do volunteer work every month, but not for a guy who makes money from it. I would also expect my expenses to be covered - you can bet the catering staff at a charity event will be paid so you should expect nothing else. I have heard the concept of working for free expressed as follows:

> *"In order for someone to get something for nothing, someone else must be getting nothing for something."*

And that doesn't sound very fair, does it?

It might be that you can see circumstances where performing at a particular venue will bring you to new audiences you would otherwise not have access to. If this is your desire, make sure you'll have the opportunity to get the word out as you see fit, taking advantage of the 'opportunity' on offer. Maybe you feel that after a couple of performances at no cost to prove your talent, you will be paid subsequently. There is a place for 'nothing ventured, nothing gained', but seek to satisfy yourself that this will indeed come to pass. With so many venues offering live music every night, finding a paying gig isn't hard enough to justify working for free. I would recommend investing time in improving your website and doing some networking with venue management over working for free.

How much to charge

Ah, the age-old question of how much to charge. The simplistic answer is that you are worth what the customer is willing to pay. The conventional wisdom on hitting the sweet spot is that once you have sufficient work to survive, you should aim to price such that 20% of your customers cannot afford you. There are of course many ways to establish your answer; in some circumstances, it may be helpful to list prices on your website so as to set expectations, in others it is of no help whatsoever. There are many aspects to consider.

Who is booking you? You might only want to request a charity pay your expenses, whilst a small local business might pay £200 and an investment bank £1000. Corporate functions will have a fixed budget, and I would never charge a large company less than £500 whilst expecting to be treated as a serious proposition. A wedding has a figure earmarked for entertainment, and I would aim to understand what the local competition are charging. That might require you call them to enquire about a booking yourself. You don't have to be cheaper but you should be mindful about how your cost compares, whether the service you are offering justifies it, and whether you'd be upset to lose the business for the sake of that cost differential.

If you are approached for a performance booking you have some sway over price, but if you are going to the market in search of work, you need to have your fee already in mind. It is wise to set a minimum; your time has a value, and you could be using it for any one of the other avenues in this book, or indeed catching up on well-earned sleep! Make sure you factor in travel and setup time, and figure out what the minimum you expect to be paid is. Let's say that your time is worth a minimum of the **£30 per hour** you could earn teaching. The gig will occupy two hours including travel and set up. For the purposes of the example, there are four of you in the band and you all have the same expectations. That means the booking fee should be 4 x £60, or £240. My real-world advice would be to add 25% to that to allow for some negotiation. It is not uncommon for the immediate comeback to any price quoted to be the suggestion the budget won't quite stretch that far. Less of a problem if you've started higher.

Once you are established and confident I would wholeheartedly recommend having a price, stating it, and then reasserting it even if counter-offered. I cannot walk into a supermarket and tell them how much I am willing to pay for my shopping, and so we meet in the middle. My time has a cost, and if you want it, you'll need to pay what it costs. Provided you are content to lose a job here and there, no problem. And losing work on cost has not happened to me for a very long time.

Potential Income

Potential income for performance is an awkward question to pin down but is based essentially on two things: the frequency with which you do it (and time spent so doing), and how big a crowd you're pulling in. If you become wildly successful you could be living in a hill-top house, driving fifteen cars, and the sky is pretty much the limit. But this book is about making money without being a star, so let's stay at the more functional end of things. A median hourly income for the various performance options would be as follows:

★	Playing a gig as part of a band	£75
★	Playing a solo show	£150
★	Dep	£150
★	Functions	£400
★	Busking	£30

From an accessibility point of view, you could be busking right now and making around £30 per hour, possibly more in the right location. Function work, at the opposite end of the income spectrum, is heavily weighted on weekends, and there are obviously less of those. By my reckoning given the amount of usable time there is in a week, and if we assume similar levels of attendance for each, in all likelihood the performance-only route would result in a maximum income in the £600 a week range, though that might mean only 'working' for around ten hours of the week (excluding any travel).

There are other financial opportunities to live performance beyond the hourly fees - notably sales of CDs and 'merch' in general, and the potential to direct more people toward your Internet presences. If you could sell a CD at each show, get a few dozen more people visiting your website triggering advertising income and music downloads, and a few dozen people viewing your videos on the monetised video sharing platforms you could increase your income substantially. When it comes to potential income, it is possible to busk all day, play gigs each weekday evening for a couple of hours and play a function each weekend, and doing so could net you an annual income of **£112,000 per year!** The likelihood of sustaining that is not fantastic in my judgement, but the original assessment of £600 per week equates to almost £30,000 per year, and could very easily be supplemented with some teaching and writing since very little time would be occupied by performance.

There are other advantages, in that live playing is likely to occur in the evenings and weekends, making it easy to fit in alongside other revenue generation strategies if you so wished. You could teach all day, and play all night. You could have the days free to spend with family, and in general organise your affairs around performance commitments. If you record your performances, you introduce the possibility of having CDs and DVDs for sale in your store, as well as increased revenue from all your Internet locations - more material means more page views! As always, being open to opportunity is key, and getting your name out there via your website as well as the various listing sites for musician promotions will get results. Many of the online directories are free, so adding your details to them is a no-brainer really.

Real world example

OK, confession time. I don't like playing live very much. I used to do it quite a bit, at least monthly… and for a period of time, daily. But I don't like the travelling around, the time away from family and the roughly equivalent time spent living in hotels. My bank manager isn't a big fan of the lack of stability of performance as an income - it always tended to be feast or famine, and I consider myself extremely lucky that the couple of good years I had were sufficient to carry me through the leaner couple that followed. If we're going to be completely straightforward about it, when the joke about a large pizza being more reliable than a musician when it comes to feeding a family is offered, it is a performing musician that we're thinking of.

Making a living from performance is not impossible by any means, and if you work hard at it a good income is available, but income will be irregular and it may be stressful at times. Trading in a job with a salary for that is not something I could recommend. I would, however, strongly recommend that you make performance part of your portfolio. The money is good, especially as part of your wider business. You improve your profile, create more opportunities for work and can generate additional material for sale either as recorded media or as material for Internet sites that generates an income via advertising and downloads. I'm a massive fan of making multiple income streams from a single activity, and performance can achieve that in spades, especially with the passive income from sales going forward. I still play live now, but I no longer actively seek work. I list past performance duties on my website, along with sound and video clips. I get work by recommendation or repeat business, and have contacts in local venues who have me on hand for Dep duty. I have earned up to £40,000 from performance alone, but my current income derived from playing live is as follows:

Dep (Annual)	£4800
Weddings / etc (Annual)	£4800
Total	**£9800**
Time Spent (Monthly)	~4hrs

There will be some residual income from traffic to my websites, but that is taken account of in previous sections. As an average, I undertake one Dep assignment and one function each month (winter months being busier for Dep work, and summer generally busier for functions). I tend to accept whenever I am asked as most of the work is coming from people I now consider friends.

Recording

Overview

★ ★ ★ ★ ☆   Difficulty

★ ★ ★ ☆ ☆   Cost

★ ★ ★ ★ ☆   Time Commitment

★ ★ ★ ☆ ☆   Likelihood of Success

★ ★ ★ ★ ☆   Income Potential

Required resources: Instruments, recording equipment (for recording yourself) versatility and patience.

If you want any people beyond the immediate audience at a performance to be able to hear your music, you're going to need to play really (really!) loud! As an alternative to that, you might consider recording your music for a paying audience to enjoy whenever they wish.

As with many other aspects of musicianship, we're living in something of a golden age. Go back to around the turn of the century and recording meant one of two things:

★ A poor quality 4-track (or if you were rich, 8-track) recorder, or;

★ Spending a fortune in the studio

Over the course of the last twenty years or so, recording equipment has gotten more and more affordable, and software products designed to make recording, editing and exporting the resultant music have gotten more and more intuitive, to the point that we can all produce our own music with minimal effort and financial outlay. Once you've got a computer, some software and something to connect them up with, you're pretty much good to go.

Recording yourself doesn't generate an income of itself of course, but it saves you a fortune when set against recording studio time and buying in the expertise of sound engineers, other musicians and all the other trappings of yesterday's recording methods. It can also deliver you near infinite product for sale on your website, streaming services, digital download providers and retailers, as well as offering up licensing and advertising opportunities to build your brand. A musician without music is, well, not much of a musician. And recording is so accessible today, you'd be crazy not to!

Recording with others can, of course, generate a significant income. Session musicians are working in every major city in the world every day to help build the music you love. Check out a record sleeve for a band you love. Maybe there are only three members of the band, yet you've noticed on the sleeve a cast list much longer than that. You probably hadn't even noticed the castanet player, had you? Well, she's a session musician drafted in to perform the part on the album, and she will have been paid very well for it too.

I am a huge exponent of recording as much as you possibly can. It will make you money in terms of tangible items you can sell. It will make you a better musician, and if you do all your own recording regularly you will almost by accident become appreciative of sound engineering, mixing tracks, editing and in general shaping the sounds that eventually make it for sale. You might even get to be competent at it, and have that extra string to your bow in a studio situation, whether your own or in session for another artist. Moreover, record everything. Every time you sit down to play, record yourself. You might come up with something incredible that if not captured, will be lost to the moment. It only takes a few seconds of killer music to build a foundation for a loop or short piece that could be sold easily to subscribers to a royalty-free stock music site, but more on that in the 'selling' section.

Finally, recording yourself will make you a better musician. When you play live, there is much to be said for the heat of the moment, the passion, the fight on the night. That is what makes performance so exciting, so immediate and ultimately so uniquely bound to an experience never to be repeated. But when you're laying down a track for posterity, you want it to be perfect. None of the scratches, blips, chirps, unintended harmonics, scuffs, missed notes, wrong notes, mistimed notes, irregular rhythms and bad timing. The list of things to avoid could probably be a book on its own. And if you record your practice, you're going to notice every last one of them. The bend that went a cent too sharp or stayed a couple flat that would have driven you mad for the rest of your life if it made it to the record, but if you play back your practice you can apply the polish.

Recording can leave you feeling a little exposed musically, kind of like seeing photographs of yourself or hearing yourself speak, but ultimately between performance and the recording experience, nothing will drive your improvement as a music professional faster, and the better you get, the better your potential income!

Recording Yourself

If you've never embraced home recording, you're really missing out as a musician. You're not able to create music whenever the mood takes you, to capture that amazing idea while it is still fresh in your mind, or to take advantage of pockets of time to build additional revenue streams. As a musician finished music is your product - think of yourself as a store; you can't make any money if you have nothing to sell, and without well-stocked shelves will anyone come in off the street to check you out? Probably not. You NEED to get into recording!

Happily, a home studio is well within reach. As with everything else in the world, you can get a functional result very cheaply indeed, and you can spend a fortune buying only the very best of everything - with the best position ideally being somewhere between the two. At the bargain basement end of the market, almost everyone has a computer, laptop, tablet, or possibly all three. If you don't, you probably have a mobile phone. Free software is available for all platforms - not as fully featured as some of the pricier options as you'd imagine, but it is functional enough to produce listenable music. A microphone or similar instrument interface is available for around the cost of a monthly cell phone bill, and that might very well be the only thing you need to purchase to start recording your music. If you don't have one, get one as soon as possible.

It is advisable to start small with recording. There is a frankly ludicrous quantity of equipment for a baffling array of purposes you have probably never heard of - I certainly hadn't. It is easy to become fixated with cool new toys at the expense of the intended outcome - spending all day playing with dials rather than recording anything. Again, been there myself! Once we move beyond the really bare essentials for a home recording studio, a more functional minimum would be:

- ★ A Computer
- ★ An Audio Interface
- ★ DAW (Digital Audio Workstation) Software
- ★ Studio Monitors
- ★ Headphones
- ★ A Microphone
- ★ A stand and filter for the microphone
- ★ A desk and a chair

The computer you've already got will more than likely be sufficient. As with every other computer purpose, the faster it is the better. Personally, I like Apple products a great deal, although they can be pricey. That said, I currently use a five-year-old machine in the heart of my recording and they are readily available on the used market.

An audio interface is likely to take the form of a powered box connecting your computer to your input source - microphone, guitar, keyboard and so on. Spending more generally yields a larger array of inputs and a facility to manipulate them, as well as potentially more intelligence within the unit to improve performance. The other differentiating factor may be software choice - the software product you use to record send edit your music, also known as DAW, often comes bundled with an audio interface. It is easier from a compatibility point of view to buy both together since you can be reasonably assured the combination of products will work, but it does limit choice and may in some cases be less cost-effective. Again, for a musician on a budget, home recording can be an addictive experience, and sufferers often choose to upgrade their equipment. This leads to a buoyant used market, and a reasonably wide choice of models from last year that work perfectly well but are available at a fraction of the cost of the slightly shinier model just announced.

When it comes to DAW products, there are three big players in town: Pro Tools, Logic and Ableton. The ins and outs of each are intricate enough that they have spawned many books in their own right, and anyone who has experience of all three has a favourite, possibly even a favourite for a particular recording or producing scenario. If you are a novice interested in a quick recommendation, it is often said that Pro Tools is best for recording, Logic is best for production and Ableton is the popular choice of DJs. That is not to say any of them are poor performers, and many would disagree with the assessment. With personal experience of them all and several others besides, my recommendation would be Logic. As well as having a huge array of virtual instruments to help you create a complete musical work, the interface is intuitive, and the help and guidance material comprehensive. You will spend the majority of your time editing and arranging so prioritising the product with the most features in that space is sensible. Logic is also very similar to Garageband, which is available for free on all Apple platforms (if you wanted to give it a trial run before jumping in with both feet). The files exported by Garageband can be read by Logic as well, providing a path between the two.

A set of speakers, or studio monitors, give you an honest an impression of your finished piece. It is impossible to recreate the playback circumstances of your future audience, but studio monitors are designed to provide as neutral a frequency response as possible to give the best approximation of an everyman speaker as possible. Personally, I favour Mackie products - they have monitors at every price point, and I find them a match for any alternative I've encountered so far. As we breeze past monitoring, think again about how you consume music. It will be worth checking playback sounds appropriately balanced through computer speakers to take account of Internet platforms and social media sharing, as well as headphones to account for those favouring MP3 players and their phones.

Headphones for use during recording are of two types for two distinct purposes: closed back for tracking and isolation, and open back to provide the best environment possible for mixing. You probably have closed back headphones already, and those headphones will probably do the job adequately. A pair of open-backed headphones, though a luxury when starting out, are a worthwhile investment toward quality recording results.

Microphones are another subject on which volumes have been written, and if you gathered 20 people to ask which was the best you'd likely get 30 answers! In summary for starting out a large diaphragm condenser microphone is good for vocals, whereas a small diaphragm condenser microphone is good for acoustic guitars, pianos and other high-frequency instruments. Any instrument with an output can likely be connected directly to your audio interface, so that's electric guitar or bass and keyboards dealt with. Drums are difficult to mic properly (in my experience), and unless you are a drummer it is more likely in a home situation you'll be adding virtual drums via software. If you are a drummer, I know plenty who rave about Shure microphones, so that would be a good place to start. When it comes to stands and filters for microphones, cheap, stable and reliable are good places to start. As with everything else they can become massively expensive for no obvious reason, though aficionados of the solid gold 'standymicscreen' will tell you it is beyond compare I am sure.

contacts that will land you paid work. I've been very lucky to have had a great session musician as a mentor, and in my early days his word was sufficient to score me a job. Once the job is secure, confidence and skill get it delivered. 'Fake it until you make it' is a good summary in that you need that swagger to pull off some of the situations in which you might find yourself, but you cannot fake the talent required to actually pull it off. Or at least you couldn't in the old days. Once again, step in Mr. Internet!

Many collaborations now happen without the participants ever meeting - I've taken on a few projects from other musicians who have commissioned me to blast a solo in the right spot on their track. They send me what they have, and maybe some notes on the kind of feel they're looking for. I'll respond with something I feel fits the track, perhaps echoing the vocal lines to some extent to build on an existing motif. Maybe I'll do a 'cut 2' for my amusement where I just go nuts and enjoy myself, and play a few fills here and there to tie the piece together. A track that has no lead guitar until it suddenly has a load of lead guitar might not feel very authentic, and it needs to feel like a continuous piece - like we could have all been in the room together recording it in one take. Even if in reality we were separated by oceans, continents and time zones. You can secure that kind of work from your existing published music, and somebody else digging what you're doing. I have never sought out such collaborations, but the requests come pretty regularly. And they're fantastic fun, as well as being very little effort and taking little time. They also become additional credits on my website and give me more experience in all respects.

The best way to get session work is to play with as many people as you can. Physically or virtually, live or in the studio, building relationships will underpin your success. Working day in, day out with people gives you time to prove you're calm in pressure situations as well as being able to deliver in them. Being reliable and punctual as well as passing the 'was I good enough for this job?' test are minimum expectations for any session musician. The more meaningful measure is 'would these people be likely to recommend me to their network of contacts?'. Would they put their reputations on the line on the strength of my work with them, confident that I will deliver? And if you can build those quality professional relationships, you will never be short of work. If your work is first rate and you make an effort to treat everyone decently, you will have no difficulty building those relationships.

As always, use your personal network, website and social media to let people know that you're available. Old school options like putting up posters or cards at local studios can work, as can listing yourself and your services on Gig Salad and all the other similar online directories for working musicians. Seek them out with your favourite search engine.

Music Production

The term 'producer' means different things to different people, and a big reason for that can be people who call themselves producers providing different services, bringing their unique combinations of skills to the studio in service of others. The term 'producer' to me means anybody taking a raw recorded signal and moving it toward a publishable result worthy of a paying public. A producer is part sound engineer, part master of technology, part mixer, part visionary and very likely a very competent musician. And if you've taken the advice throughout this book to gather a basic set of tools to work in all those spaces, it could well end up being a good description for you!

Producers are often thought of as the virtuosos of the studio as an instrument, building sonic masterpieces by selecting and coaching the musicians, influencing arrangements and ultimately shaping the resultant sound. For the musician looking to make money from production, I consider the real money making opportunities to exist post-recording. It is not time or cost efficient for you to spend a day in the studio working on recording somebody else's record. In today's technologically evolved world, it is possible to gather all the recording output from a studio session, load it into a computer and build a track with a mixture of that material and virtual instruments.

Once you're all set up with a studio for your own recording projects, and you've learned how to efficiently pilot your tools and workflow through to a polished end result, you have acquired skills in demand to others. The vast majority of people who play want to record, and the vast majority of those who attempt to record have developed inadequate skills for their ultimate purpose - to produce a track that is of sufficient quality to distribute. The majority of aspiring musicians do not think further ahead than mastery of their craft, or more specifically their instrument. A few build on that to an understanding that their band needs to function as a unit to produce a top-quality outcome. Still fewer consider how they will capture their sound and make it available to audiences beyond the venue. We're back to building as broad a skill base as possible so as to be useful to as many people as possible.

There are many ways to make money as an independent music producer, but the easiest start is with producing for your friends and those in your professional network. It is not what you know, but who you know. Your own recorded material is your most effective business card, so make sure your available recordings are the best you can possibly make them. You can then give your clients a personal service as well as a professional one, firstly because you know them, but secondly because you are not a pro studio. That is sometimes presented as a negative but it is all about how you use it to your advantage.

The stereotypical professional studio will be a pretty bland space, with pretty uncomfortable furnishings, serving sub-standard tea in Styrofoam cups. Sounds great huh? The balance shifts slightly when the pro studio includes an enormous desk lifted from a spaceship, every microphone known to man and connectivity from anything, to anything. But the reality is that only the top studios boast a comprehensive array of useful technology, and unless you are independently wealthy or backed by a big record company, those are not the studios in which you will find yourself. The kit you have in a home studio is a lot closer to that available to the man in the street in a standard studio than you would imagine. And it will not surprise you to hear that a top producer running your rig would probably get an incredible result out of it all the same, whilst your result from his best in class studio setup is likely to sound less polished in comparison. Embrace what you've got, and learn how to use it well, you have after all got exactly the same digital audio workstation software at the heart of your setup as all the big guys have in theirs.

The next rung on this ladder once you have produced tracks for friends and your professional circle could be virtual collaboration. As we discovered in the previous section on work as a session musician, technology has made it possible to work with other artists and musicians without ever setting eyes on them, or sharing the same physical space. The same applies to production. Armed with recorded material and your computer, you can create something truly mesmerising. Make sure to include production services on your website if you want to offer them - it ties in nicely with the ability to offer virtual session musician services, since you would want to work on your raw recorded track to make it as polished as possible without sending it back. And once you've amassed the skills necessary to work on your own music, you might as well use those skills to make money from others. It is a sensible and efficient use of your talents and can make a meaningful contribution to your income.

Standard fees for production are massively variable, perhaps unsurprisingly given that no two producers are bringing the same set of skills to the party, and if you're working with the bigger players, contracts can get pretty complicated... but that's probably for another book. For those starting out, there are four basic ways to get paid:

★ An advance - an amount of money paid to the producer before the process starts to secure support for the duration. Usually based on experience and reputation, and recoupable against future royalties.

★ A Fund Deal - Production fees may be included in overall studio costs if using your own.

★ A Flat rate - often used for post-production and virtual work, with £200 per track being typical amongst my network.

★ Royalties.

The first three in that run down are pretty self-explanatory: an agreed amount of money is paid to the producer in return for their services. Royalties are interesting though - the producer will get a percentage of the artist royalty for a record, which to simplify means the producer gets around 33p every time a CD gets sold. And between three and five percent of next to nothing for each stream over a network.

Producers get what is known as 'record one royalties', which is to say that whilst an artist does not receive any income from sales of their music until all recording fees have been recovered, a producer makes money from the very first sale. That income might be delayed by 'retroactive record one', which means the producer will not receive any income until all recording fees have been recovered, but at that point the producer is due all royalties from the very first sale.

Fundamentally, all these agreements are made ahead of time, and chances are you're not going to break through immediately and be working on the kind of production gigs where you need to concern yourself with record one, advances and such. My production work has been mostly for flat fees, but I've always sought to arrange a royalty payment. They're actually pretty useful in independent circles since costs have to be kept low and all income is artist income in the majority of cases. This means that although sales volumes might be lower, you're looking at a percentage of the sale revenue rather than a percentage of the artist percentage once all costs have been recovered. I am happy to reduce my flat fee in return for an ongoing income from royalties, and I find it can strengthen working relationships as well. Having some skin in the game, and a vested interest in the best possible outcome, can eliminate any concern around working your hours for a flat fee and doing a job that is 'good enough'. It will be apparent to all that we're shooting for the best possible end product to secure the best ongoing result for the whole group. Not just working for the money.

There are, as always, a multitude of companies online who can promote your services to an existing audience, securing you work on the strength of your past accomplishments or existing catalogue. Simply register, complete your bio, provide examples of your work and wait for the work to roll in! Most specialise in virtual engagements where the participants never meet, but some maintain geographical directories as well, providing access to local and available music professionals.

Potential Income

Potential income from recording and subsequently distributing your own music is covered in the section on selling music coming up soon, with this section making reference only to the recording process. Income from sessions, like income from teaching, is based to a significant extent on how much time you spend doing it. Meteoric rises to superstardom within the session field are unlikely, since your very definition is to play second-fiddle to 'the talent': the person paying for your time.

If we assume a 40-hour working week and 48-week year, and take the union rate of £31 for planning purposes, that would mean a full-time studio musician income of **£59520 per year!** Once again, not too shabby for a career noted for its inability to feed a family! That indicative figure becomes much healthier when we remember the union fee, though standard for broadcast media, is often eclipsed by some margin, with £100 per hour being far from uncommon. So a real income for a full-time session musician could easily reach into six figures!

Until relatively recently session musicians were paid an agreed fee for their time, and regardless of how big the recorded work got, or their meaningful contribution to it, that initial fee was all they would ever receive. There are some very famous records out there that have grossed millions, yet the musicians responsible for them might only have been paid for the hour they spent doing it: £31 at union rate. That all started changing in 1996 with an EU directive demanding equitable remuneration for all performers when a piece of music is played on the radio. Finally, session musicians see a reward in relation to the success of the track in question. Membership of the Performing Rights Society (PRS), Performing Artists Media Rights Association (PAMRA) and the Phonographic Performance Limited (PPL) organisations is an enabler for royalty recovery in the UK. Membership of a musician's union is a pre-requisite for some work (notably in broadcast media), as well as any session paying union rates being likely to require union membership. The Musician's Union is the UK union, offering membership tiers matched to income bands. I have found membership worthwhile as the union provides legal advice for free to its members. The American Federation of Musicians of the United States and Canada (AFM) is the equivalent on the other side of the pond.

Real world example

I think we can agree that working full-time as a session musician carries with it around the same level of likelihood as hitting it big in any other respect. You would need either one very solid gig, like playing in the house band for a national TV show for instance, or a network of contacts sufficient to provide you with near full-time work. In so doing you would be a professional musician (no doubt about that) but when we set out ultimately in search of freedom, what we would have found would be a full-time job.

Making a good living from recording is not impossible by any means, and if you work hard at it a good income is available, but income from session work is likely to be irregular and it may be stressful at times. Trading in a job with a salary for that is not something I could recommend. I would recommend that you make session work part of your portfolio. The money is good, especially as part of your wider business. You improve your profile, create more opportunities for work and can generate additional material for sale, either as recorded media or as material for Internet sites that generates an income via advertising and downloads. I'm a massive fan of making multiple income streams from a single activity and recording can achieve that in spades, especially with the passive income from production jobs on sales going forward, and from radio play royalties derived from recording credits. I get work by recommendation or repeat business, having built a network of people with whom I like to work, and who seem to like working with me. I have earned up to £30,000 per year from hourly recording fees, as well as a 5 figure income from production. You will see from the below that producing music for others is more lucrative, since a percentage of the artist fee on sales is worth significantly more in monetary terms than the hourly fees associated with the studio sessions. Best of all, 75% of the production income is royalties, meaning it will continue to come at no cost in terms of my time. My current income derived from recording is as follows:

Studio Sessions (Annual)	£5,000
Production, inc. royalties (Annual)	£9,000
Total	**£14,000**
Time Spent (Monthly)	~38hrs

There will be some residual income from traffic to my websites, but that is taken account of in previous sections. Similar to Dep, I do not seek out session work anymore, but if it finds me I am very happy to do it. I enjoy being an active music professional, and being able to exercise my chops - demonstrating I've still got it, is worthwhile personally, professionally and financially.

Selling your Music

Overview

★ ★ ★ ★ ☆ Difficulty

★ ★ ☆ ☆ ☆ Cost

★ ★ ☆ ☆ ☆ Time Commitment

★ ★ ★ ☆ ☆ Likelihood of Success

★ ★ ★ ★ ★ Income Potential

Required resources: Your instruments and recording equipment, a group of like-minded people (if appropriate) and a paying audience!

Not signed to a major label? Don't worry about it! Of all the artists that are signed, well over 90% fail. If you take into account the odds of getting discovered, getting signed and being successful we're well into the territory of being struck by lightning holding a jackpot-winning lottery ticket, a year to the day since exactly the same thing happened! It is much more realistic and achievable to learn the ropes of the music business yourself. You get to retain control of your intellectual property (your music, brand, and image) and retain a much greater percentage of sales profits. If you fund everything yourself, or 'bootstrap' as it is known in business, you can easily control the associated costs and risks, managing the possibility of failure. Costs can be kept low with commission driven deals, and on demand CD creation can reduce your need to hold stock.

Once upon a time, independent musicians would record their music, sell it via mail order and small local record shops, and hope to be discovered by happy accident one day. For many, that day was a long time coming, whilst for most it never came at all - we're back to that musician versus a large pizza thing again. Today the big acts that we've all heard of make the majority of their money from touring and merchandising, and you'll have probably noticed almost all the record shops have disappeared. When is the last time you physically got a CD out of a case and hit play?

It is said that it is harder to make money from music today than ever, and it is certainly true that the return per unit sold is lower than in years gone by. It is, however, also true that it has never been easier to share your music with the world, and access to the global listener market has never been easier or more immediate. Gone are the days of mail order cassettes and begging independent record store for a spot on the shelf. With a few well-placed clicks, you can get your music listed on all the download sites and available to a paying public.

The Internet has made it possible for everyone to reach millions of potential fans from around the world for between low and no cost. The biggest obstacle is getting their attention in the first place. The ease of access is fantastic for the big-name artists and their labels who can invest a fortune to ensure they grasp that attention. You can get your voice heard by launching your website, marketing through social media, setting up an online store, and distributing your music to all the major music retailers in minutes; all for an extremely low cost. Artists now have control, should they wish to exercise it. Never before has it been so simple to reach your potential market.

Digital download of full tracks is not the only way to monetise music of course. Previous sections have referenced the use of your own website to sell physical items and digital downloads, as well as using advertising to monetise video. The Internet age has introduced a myriad of options for getting your music out to the world, and you will have spotted that diversification is key to success in music, particularly while we're waiting for the big time!

Selling on your Website

Sales of music have grown exponentially in the digital age. Somewhat disappointingly however, income from music sales for the artist is decreasing thanks largely to the reduction in physical CD sales. The change in listener behaviour means that individual tracks are typically purchased rather than albums, and the cut the digital music and streaming platforms take on sales has an impact on income. You can take some of the sting out of that by being your own middleman, selling your music direct to a paying public.

Setting up a store on your website if you went with the WordPress recommendation is as simple as installing and configuring a plugin. Over and above this, plugins for music downloads are available which allow you to protect your digital downloads. These will allow you to set up like a big-time Internet record store with the means to list all your music for sale as digital downloads. From there customers will be able to make purchases, payments will be made and verified before being sent directly to your digital payment or bank account. The customer gets a unique download link - this is important to maintain your revenue stream and the integrity of your work. Were the download link not unique, nothing would stop one customer sharing it with all their friends, really hurting your bottom line.

If setting that up sounds like a lot of work and you don't want to have to pay a guy, there are several services available that will automate it all for you, providing the same functions as above in return for a membership fee. They will list all your music, process payments and ensure customer downloads are controlled and secure. All you have to do is upload your music and cover art, and name your price. You're already on your way to understanding brand and marketing if you're working your own website, social media, and promotional materials, and the single most important thing is engagement with your audience. Get in touch with them, communicate with them regularly and let them know what's new. Once you get the word out for a new record hopefully you're gathering interest long before it is ready for release.

Selling physical CDs and DVDs is probably best done face to face at performances where possible to maximise the potential for additional sales, as well as removing the overhead of dealing with postage, but the sale of physical items is simple via a website, using the e-commerce facilities available through WordPress. Again, there are several Internet companies who will cut CDs on demand and post them direct to customers on order. They take such a huge percentage of the sale price that I can't recommend using them until you get to the point that the income is no more than a bonus for no effort. Invest in a run and ship your own CDs; I bet it doesn't become a problem you need to fix. Think about how you consume music today.

To that end, it is wise to offer as many purchasing options as possible. Once you have your music available with the digital platforms, it makes sense to link to your music from your website. The digital platforms offer affiliate programs which you can join, and they will provide instructions for listing products. Should a visitor to your site purchase one of these products, you'll get a commission paid. Music sales sites such as CDBaby, iTunes, and Amazon all offer affiliate services, and if you link to your own music from your store pages to provide your visitors with options, you will get commission on the sale as well thereby increasing your income!

Selling with the digital platforms

Though I have repeatedly demonstrated my appreciation for a good website, and would always advocate you sell your music direct to maximise income, I also think it is important to give your audience choice. Linking to your music on the various digital music stores allows them to do what works best for them and their devices. Sure, you won't make as much money from the sale, and you can even make that clear on the page, but better to get 70% of a sale than 100% of nothing if they leave your site empty-handed.

Many music consumers today do not get any further than the digital download stores associated with their music players. It is possible to list your music with some of these organisations yourself, which means registering as a record label. This may be worthwhile if you envision selling a great deal of music via the platforms, but the process is reasonably lengthy and complex, with no guarantee of success. It is also impossible to register with some providers without a distributor.

As a first foray into digital music sales, use of an aggregator is recommended unless you want to encode, produce, curate and manage your catalogue. I am usually a big exponent of doing things yourself or at least learning how, but I'm happy to make an exception on this one. The administrative overhead of doing your own digital music company interactions would be time much better spent elsewhere.

For a nominal fee, the aggregator companies will format and deliver your music to the right specifications, ensuring that it is uploaded correctly. They will also provide you with the various product codes you need to distribute your music across multiple channels, as well as taking care of all of that for you with a few mouse clicks. The digital music companies pay the aggregator for any sales, and the aggregator then pays you as the content owner. Without an aggregator you get the pleasure of doing all of that yourself, though 'pleasure' is not the word I'd use having attempted it. Most of the aggregation companies work on either a flat rate per track or album, or a commission. The commission route keeps initial costs extremely low, but the flat rate gives a better return over the long term, your choice based largely on whether you can fund the flat rate payment, and whether you believe sales volumes justify it.

The big advantage of using a digital music aggregator is the fact they'll deal with all the music platforms for you, where you would need to repeat the registration process with each in turn, and manage your music catalogue with each independently. If you thought doing it once was hard work, imagine doing the same thing half a dozen times! The aggregators also operate qualifying criteria for the artists and music they accept, so make sure your recordings are good quality and your cover art similarly professional to stand the best chance of meeting the requirements.

Should you find yourself falling short of aggregator expectations, all is not lost. Several specialist distributors are out there, who for a flat rate will encode your music and make it available across all the major digital platforms. And their rates are pretty reasonable too; from as little as £1 a track with you retaining all rights and royalties. Not a bad deal if you ask me. All you need to do is sign up, upload your music and cover art and you're good to go!

Royalty-free (Stock) Music

We have discussed the ability for a modern musician to make money from sharing video, images and Internet content in general by monetising with advertising. More or less every video you've ever watched on a video sharing platform has music, and the video sharing sites do not allow the use of copyrighted material without redirecting all advertising revenue to the copyright holder. So everyone who ever shares a video on any subject who wishes to monetise it needs royalty-free music. Music can be offered royalty-free under license (see next section), but it is also possible to earn a good income by composing and providing tracks to reseller platforms specialising in royalty-free music.

You make have heard of 'stock images'; pictures made available for commercial re-use by their creators for a one-off fee. You could be producing 'stock music' for use in Internet video, TV ads, computer games, promotional materials and much more. People looking for royalty-free music to accompany their work are plentiful, and they're looking for just about everything from the simplest drum loop or guitar riff to full choral pieces, orchestral opuses and everything in between. The larger organisations may have relationships with artists, studios and record companies, and have access to music via various means. For mere mortals, or independents just like us, music library Internet sites are often the easiest way to find quality music at affordable prices.

It is possible to make a very good income from any finished piece of music, regardless of length, up to a point. You will find advice in the recording section to get into the habit of recording yourself all the time, even during practice. You may find a melody, that once a drum loop and an underlying bass line has been added would not be out of place as a backing groove for a corporate promo video. And all you had to do was take the 30-second clip you already had, spend ten minutes editing it, and upload it to the music library site. We should all be big on extracting maximum value from our time and resources - so re-use of material is job number one for all of us.

Instrumental loops can be uploaded with modest variation in tempo, pitch, length and underlying rhythm to create several separate and distinct stock music products for customer download. Full tracks can also be offered for royalty-free download. Some of the stock music sites require exclusivity, whilst others will go as far as commissioning you to create tracks for them to sell to their customers. The best approach is the one that is best for you, personally I diversify and direct my product in all available directions:

★ Exclusivity typically pays most in percentage terms, some up to 65%, but you need to ensure the site you choose can get you the sales. It is best to push 'pop' material in this direction.

★ Upload the bulk of your royalty-free music to sites that do not demand exclusivity. These will pay between 35% and 50% typically but you are likely to see more downloads.

★ Write tracks on commission if the fee offered makes it worthwhile to you. Fees are often in the region of £500 per track, but the tracks need to be professional and generally include vocals. Frankly, such a track is to my mind worth more sold directly from your website and the digital platforms.

Being successful with stock music relies on being as mainstream as possible within your genre, so whilst all the fringes of the industry are represented, the more esoteric your music is, the fewer people it will appeal to and thus the fewer sales you are likely to secure. This is not a world that rewards creative excess, the goal is almost to create as inoffensive a background as possible for a broader piece of work the customer needs a musical contribution for. The music in these settings is typically not centre-stage. With that in mind, if you're going to go this route, compose music specifically for the purpose - you can still come up with a fantastic hard rock riff and back it up with some killer drums, but if you come away from the edit believing you've got something really fantastic you might want to head toward the paid digital download sites, retaining royalties, rather than letting it go for a few pounds or dollars.

Stock music is provided to the customer royalty-free for a one-off cost, and almost always without attribution, meaning if you take this route you may be unaware where your music has been used and who by. The listener will also be unaware that the music they can hear has been produced by you. The reward for stock music is purely financial at the point of sale; whilst some passive income is possible in terms of a track being downloaded for months to come, delivering a fee each time, no payments are associated with the volume of airplay the completed work receives. If the standard download fee for your track is £34, and your cut is £17, it is £17 you will receive whether your music was used in a home movie that nobody watched, or a cinema trailer for a Hollywood blockbuster. Royalty-free is royalty-free.

No Money Music

'Whoa…. Hold on there! I thought we were looking to make money here?'… I hear you, and we are, but recorded music is just one of many streams making up an income for a modern musician, and there is a time and a place for a good freebie. Don't panic, there's something in it for you!

Sales funnels have become well known in marketing circles. Operating in tiers, the idea is to start with an offering that the majority of potential customers will have interest in and very little resistance toward, thereby gathering as many people as possible for the rest of the journey. The next phase asks the customer for a little more in terms of engagement and potentially payment, but at this point you're working with an audience you know are interested in you and your products. Some will turn out to have been interested enough for the first phase, but not enough for the second… and that's cool. When you move on to the next stage you will have a group of people who have stuck with you and demonstrated an ongoing commitment to your music. Now is your opportunity to sell your big ticket item, knowing that the people still with you are amongst the most likely to go for it.

So we're after an introductory tier, which should appeal to anyone and everyone, whilst offering no barriers to engagement. And we need to get the word out. Here is a great place for some free music! You could simply drive around in your car throwing CDs out of the window, or go nuts and make all your digital downloads free, but what we're looking for here is encouraging engagement with you as an artist, with a view to future sales. We need to be more thoughtful and specific.

You could offer free downloads on your website, perhaps to new subscribers via a newsletter to reward them, or perhaps to people signing up at a particular show. You could use download codes specific to flyers handed out at specific events, which make a particular downloadable item free. All are great ways to engage with your fan base and keep them interested in you, and likely to result in a subset of them paying for an additional product.

Rather than just giving your music away for free, assign Creative Commons licensing. Creative Commons allows you to provide your music for others to download and use as they see fit, subject to conditions you specify. Those conditions relate to:

★ Attribution: Others can copy, distribute, display, perform and remix your music if they credit you as you have requested. **(BY)**

★ No Derivative Works: specifies that your music can be copied, distributed, displayed and performed only in its original form. **(ND)**

★ Share Alike: Your music can only be shared by others on the same terms under which you shared it with them. **(SA)**

★ Non-Commercial: Others can copy, distribute, display, perform and remix your music only for non-commercial purposes. **(NC)**

Over a billion works are protected by Creative Commons licensing worldwide, and whilst any music made available for download under such arrangements could be considered your gift to the world, it also represents an opportunity to reach new audiences. There are loads of sites out there that specialise in Creative Commons and free to use music - Jamendo and Frostwire being two I use myself (others are available via your preferred search engine). Upload your music to them and provide all your information so you can be properly credited as you wish to be.

'But how am I making money from this?', I hear you cry... and we're almost there. More or less every video you've ever watched on a video sharing platform has music, and the video sharing sites do not allow the use of copyrighted material without redirecting all advertising revenue to the copyright holder. So everyone who ever shares a video on any subject who wishes to monetise it needs royalty-free music - let them use yours in return for properly crediting you. People will hear the music, see you credited, find your website and in this simple act, become potential fans who otherwise would not have found you. Or even have known to look.

You get bonus points here for thinking far enough ahead that you've removed the vocal from each of your existing tracks and released the instrumental versions for download under Creative Commons. Maybe you'd prefer to release a verse and chorus section for use as a music loop. The people who came to find your website because they enjoyed the instrumental rock driving in the background of that skateboarding video in which you were credited are extremely likely to pay 99p to download the full track. You will also pick up some followers on social media and email addresses for your mailing list. Most importantly we're getting people into that first stage of the funnel, engaged with you for low or no cost and already more likely to buy one of your records than they were before. Cool!

Potential Income

Potential income from sales of recorded music is another area where if you do manage to hit the jackpot by becoming wildly successful you could be partying with the biggest names, mixing single malt with coke without a second thought, and the world is your oyster. But this book is about making money without being a star, so let's keep our feet on the ground a bit here. Typical income per unit from the various distribution options is as follows:

★ Selling a CD direct - £ the price, less approx. £2 for production

★ Selling digital direct - £ the price you charge

★ Selling a PoD CD - £3

★ Selling digital via resellers - approx. 30% of the retail price

★ A stream of a single track - a penny (!)

As you can plainly see, selling directly from your website sees the greatest percentage of your sale income make it to your pocket. The eternal question is whether you're going to sell a hundred via your website, but a million via digital resellers. 100% of one hundred sales at £10 each nets you £1,000. 30% of a million sales, even at a pound each, would deliver £300,000, which is precisely why both options are advantageous. It makes no sense to close yourself off from any potential avenue. Even at a penny a stream, a lucky break with a shared video or social media interaction can result in massive volumes of listeners - suddenly a series of slow drips becomes a mighty river!

There are other financial opportunities associated with having saleable music beyond the direct income - notably raising the profile of your brand as a musician, and creating interest in your work. That interest translates readily into more people heading toward your Internet presences. Major labels, venue proprietors, and agents are much more likely to find you and consider you as a proposition if you're established, with music well publicised and an engaged fan base (regardless of size). If you could sell a CD or two each week, get a few dozen more people visiting your website thereby triggering advertising income and music downloads, and a few dozen more people viewing your videos as well as those of others that use and credit your music on the monetised video sharing platforms, your income could increase substantially.

Some of the best-selling artists famously make millions of pounds with a single release, never mind within a year. Even for the famous few, the likelihood of sustaining that is not fantastic, and I believe an income of a few hundred pounds a month is a realistic minimum for working purposes. You might win big, but who can say? I can tell you from my own experience that a couple of CDs worth of music can make you several thousand pounds a year.

Real world example

It will not surprise you if you've read any of the other sections in this book to hear that I, like most working musicians, make money from several distinct flavours of music sales. I sell physical CDs in relatively modest numbers, usually direct from my website, and whilst I used to invest in print and duplication runs myself to maximise profit, I no longer have time for the associated effort. Processing orders, dealing with postage and returns and so forth is work I do not need. I am now very happy to let another company deal with the sales. They receive the order, create the CDs as necessary and ship them direct to the customer.

Digital downloads are simple. I registered my company with the main player in this space many many years ago, when it was much easier to do so, and I deal with them directly. I use a content aggregator for all the others as it is quicker and easier, all I have to do is upload my music and cover art, provide a price and press a button. I then list all my digital downloads on my own Internet sites, as well as using my affiliate links for the platforms to maximise my income. It only adds a couple of pennies to the income from each download, but if it is my money, I'll have it thank you very much.

Royalty-free music has made me very happy over the years! I was at a stage financially where a bird in the hand was worth two in the bush, as the saying goes - I had a choice of several thousand pounds in my hand right now, or the prospect of a little more money overall, delivered in smaller instalments over time. I needed the money, so I opted for the former by providing the music to a major broadcaster on a royalty-free basis. Ordinarily, my recommendation would be to retain your rights and protect future income, and there is no doubt I lost money in the longer term with this decision. But since I was buying a house and needed the money, it remains the best decision I could have made. Best of all, the music itself was the result of practice sessions over the course of a few months, appropriately polished with additional instrument tracks for a rounded result. I have earned up to £60,000 annually from music sales alone, but last year's income was as follows:

Royalty-free music	£17,000
CD Sales (Annual)	£2,000
Digital Downloads (Annual)	£4,000
Total	**£23,000**
Time Spent (Monthly)	~40hrs

As you might reasonably expect of a musician, the majority of my working time is spent playing, and I record everything I play. I spend two hours each week on average uploading music to the various content providers, the rest of the time indicated above on manipulating tracks for use under royalty-free or Creative Commons arrangements. The latter having no easily attributable income in monetary terms. This income alone could be sufficient to sustain the majority of sensible lifestyles, as well as making a very good contribution towards a sillier one!

Composing

Overview

★ ★ ★ ★ ☆ Difficulty

★ ★ ☆ ☆ ☆ Cost

★ ★ ★ ☆ ☆ Time Commitment

★ ★ ★ ☆ ☆ Likelihood of Success

★ ★ ★ ☆ ☆ Income Potential

Required resources: Instruments and recording equipment, a pile of manuscript paper, good music theory knowledge, the ability to write music and a ton of patience!

The advances made in the modern music world are great news for pretty much all types of musician, and almost all professions in the music industry have benefited as a consequence. Musical scores have, for everyone beyond musicians, become almost a curiosity. Since the score was the only place one was likely to note a composer, their level of exposure has taken a hit with the decrease in interest. Composers today are less well known that they were centuries ago, with fewer chances for fame and fortune. There are, however, several ways to make an income from composition. Many of them are extremely accessible, low cost, or are possible as add-ons to work you're already doing. I'm a huge exponent of arranging things so you can get paid more than once with the same piece of time and effort, and composition is a fantastic example of that working model.

You might not consider yourself a composer, but if you're writing your own music or arranging that of others, that is exactly what you are doing! It is admittedly a pretty big leap to get from there to becoming a big-time composer for Hollywood blockbuster movies or the go-to songwriter for pop music's hottest act this year, but the accessibility of technology and ease with which your work can be shared with a global audience are fantastic news for the independent. If you've set yourself up with a basic home studio, you have the means to produce output that can rival that of the biggest names. You have access to the same tools, and could potentially even be learning from these people directly from material online.

An understanding of music structure is a must-have for any aspiring composer. You're not going to get far writing music if you don't know how to hang a song together. Formal education is a huge advantage as well, those dry music theory lessons you suffered as a child could finally pay off! It is said that 10,000 hours of practice are required to become a master of a given craft, so if you start now, and put eight hours a day into it every single day, you could be there in just three and a half years! More seriously, that 10,000-hour figure can be eaten in to pretty well with all the exposure to music you've had through the years. Listening to music for a lifetime bestows upon us all a basic understanding of rhythm and song structure. You probably understood cadences before you knew what they were; if you still don't, it's the way music resolves (or doesn't) to sound complete before going around again, and is the reason you might have a very good idea which note is coming next even if you've never heard a piece before. On top of that, you've been playing an instrument for long enough to be considering how you can make money from it which is again a significant skill. You would absolutely benefit from some time in a classroom specifically on composition, but it is also possible to learn whilst working. You can start small and only start entertaining bigger jobs when your skills and experience make them possible.

A composer today is often not like the picture you have in your head of a guy in a powdered wig sat in front of a piano with some paper and a quill, teasing out a note at a time, though I'm sure there are many who do figure pieces out and scribble them down in that sort of fashion. A composer today is more likely to be sitting at a computer with DAW software running and writing music, scoring and syncing that music to the demands of the customer - film music, for instance, will need crescendos in certain places to match the on-screen action. The majority of composers today who are working independently will make extensive use of samples and library music. It isn't until you get to the biggest of films with the biggest of budgets that you would be likely to find a composer working with musicians in real time.

Although an incredibly competitive field at the top end, with chances of success similar to those of being a big star of stage and screen, being a composer is much more accessible from the more modest side of things. As discussed in previous sections, music is everywhere, and somebody needs to create and produce all that music. Well, somebody needs to write it first as well. TV and film are the clearly big-ticket items for a composer, followed by songwriting for pop acts who focus on their image and their dancing, but often not so much their songwriting talent. They understand that it is best to pay someone who knows what he is doing for that bit! And whilst those are undoubtedly the places our minds go when we think of composition, and they would be the opportunities likely to make a great deal of money, there is money to be made elsewhere with a much greater likelihood of success for a composer who is just starting out. The independent circles of small film, lower budget television, commercials, corporates, local radio, video sharing sites and social media outlets are all a much more fertile ground for you or me. They are great places to make some music, make some money, and further build your skills and reputation until that big job does land at your door!

Film/ TV Composition

Working in film or TV, as we've already established, is the best way to become well known as a composer. As a film composer, you will have the budget to enable some truly awe-inspiring work using the best musicians in the business, the best facilities and the best supporting cast to help you make your masterpiece a cinematic reality. How many composers can you name right now? Some of the classical big names I'm sure; Beethoven, Mozart… but what about after that? Do you know who composed the theme for the Right Guard deodorant commercial in 1997? No, of course you don't, and neither do I. Nor does anybody else. But I'd bet you know John Williams, and you could probably hum one of his creations right now. In the interests of balance, I also have the music from that Right Guard commercial in my head now, which probably means 'that guy' did pretty well out of it too! As a composer in TV, you might not quite hit the budgets of the film studios, but you've arguably got a bigger audience and you're hitting them week after week.

The difficult part, of course, is making the transition from being the best composer in your house, to a composer with enough reputation to take that call from the major studios. Composing for a big film could make you tens of thousands of pounds, making it extremely attractive. There are plenty of books out there that will tell you to figure out how to be in the right place at the right time - basically in Los Angeles, all the time. Or you could get the details for production staff and send in demo material, your own scoring for a film to demonstrate your capability, or maybe just go and doorstep a producer? Regardless of those sorts of cold-call approaches, a magic breakthrough moment is pretty unlikely, and I won't tell you otherwise. So, whilst we wait for that particular miracle, let's look at the other things you can do to make some money at film composition.

For starters, almost all locations have a local film scene, and if yours doesn't it probably means you haven't found it yet. There will be a local group of people who are out there making moving images every day, including many independent guys who are starting out, just like you. Their budgets are not going to be huge, which could potentially be a disadvantage, and I've already said you shouldn't work for free. A caveat for that is that you shouldn't work for free unless you're really sure that vague promise of future paid work is actually going to happen, or that the promise of exposure as a result will actually distil into some paid work. And I wouldn't be sure of that if I were you. I would, however, be very happy to work in return for a share of the income from whatever the output of the venture is. Films are made for an audience - if a guy wants some music for his home movie then that's cool, and he can pay you for that, but just about any other film, no matter how small, has an audience. And an audience means it will make money. Negotiate your slice of the pie, and make sure you have that agreement written down and signed. The income might not be huge, but an extra ten quid a month could be make or break down the line. If you intend to work for modest income, I would suggest matching that with modest effort. Provide your best of course, since everything you do is a reflection of you, but look to reuse existing material - which has the added benefit of increasing sales of your wider work - the original track you have sampled, your royalty-free music collection, and so on.

The local area is good for accessibility, immediacy and the minimising of effort, but it also reduces your available audience, so get involved in the independent film circuit. As with every other interest group, there are internet forums, social media groups, and professional networking groups devoted to independent filmmaking. So get yourself involved. Once you've got some material on your website (there we go again - get a website!) you can use it as a shop front; whether it is a video, a song, a loop or anything else it is an example of your work as a composer. Yet another reason that having an eclectic selection there is extremely helpful; you want people to find something that helps them understand your range as an artist. You might also consider a specific section on your site for composition, even if you then simply duplicate a selection of your work into it - at least people looking for a composer know where to look! Get yourself out there, sign up for the various networking groups and make sure you include your website details in your setup. Be interested in people's projects; you never know where it may lead. There are events organised for filmmakers and they seem to attract a very producer-centric crowd. At the couple I have been to I have been the only composer or musician in the room, dramatically increasing my chances of finding work. Go along, have some conversations, swap some cards. Networking is absolutely the route to work here, so get out there and build some relationships. With a bit of luck, once you get to know a few people in the film circle, you can socialise and accidentally network at the same time whilst being recommended for work beyond your immediate contacts. Perfect! A middle tier film with national distribution, even if a fairly niche release, could pay between five and ten thousand pounds.

Do not overlook student film either. All the great filmmakers of tomorrow are starting to hone their craft today, and they need music too! Again, budgets can be a problem. But I've been paid sensible money, particularly by final year students, for providing music for their projects as well as for those who wish to invest in their portfolio as they start out in professional life. It is very easy to get your contact details through to local colleges and universities via faculty; cards listing you as a composer with your website printed on and a cover letter are all you'll need. The same rules of engagement as previous for working for little; make sure you're getting a future promise of something at the very least. If you are going to provide music for the love of it, reusing your existing royalty-free material is advised. There is no sense in spending time doing something and not getting paid. Finally, there may be additional benefits to working in film - I got my first appearance in film from a composition job. They needed a guy to play a private detective in a film noir, and I was there at the right time. Smoking at a desk, running down some stairs looking purposeful, checking a corpse for some papers, as well as some fairly amateurish pyrotechnics that almost ruined a perfectly good office can all now be listed on my CV with a straight face!

Video Game Composition

Video gaming is a big industry, and becoming bigger. Budgets for the big games approach those of filmmaking, with game publishers making billions from game sales worldwide. That much money in an industry makes it easier to get your share. With the industry being less well established than film it can be easier to find opportunities, but with the runaway success of video gaming and the budgets available, it can mean some big names competing for those opportunities.

Similar to work in film and TV, the difficult element of working in video game composition is crossing that line between thinking what a great idea it might be and making it happen. If you play video games yourself you will be aware that many of the big titles have almost cinematic title scores, as well as smaller pieces of music that may become familiar over time; perhaps during menu and load sequences, or when the giant end of level bad guy is about to burst through a wall and head straight for you. You could contact game studios and developers with an introductory letter or email, including some of your material as a reference point, and you might get lucky. It sadly remains likely, however, that you'll receive a polite decline or promise of contact in the future should an opportunity arise. It is still possible to make money from video gaming, but as with film, we need to look elsewhere to the routes less travelled.

Mobile games represent a phenomenal change in the games industry. Mobile games are developed at a lower cost; therefore they have smaller budgets. The lower budget demands a more modest use of resources in general, and music is no exception. The games themselves are often offered free to the player, funded by a combination of advertising revenue and in-game purchasing of new items and level packs. The requirements for music might actually align better with jingles for commercials than epic score for film; a mobile game developer needs a few notes that are evocative and ideally memorable, not a ten-minute opus. One of the biggest mobile games right now has music for the opening credits consisting of four notes, and a background theme through the play session that is a six-second melody, looped indefinitely. That sort of requirement lends itself to the royalty-free music approach of high volumes of output at a reduced duration. Perfect from the point of view of time taken to create such pieces, as well as the risk of committing your resources to gaming music rather than other fields. Additionally, new mobile games are being created every day in their hundreds, meaning that hundreds of people every day are developing games, requiring hundreds or possibly thousands of pieces of music. Every. Single. Day.

It will be no surprise to you now that I suggest pitching your composition efforts at mobile gaming as a springboard. Studios from the well-established and social media integrated giants, to Steve in his bedroom need music right now. And if they don't choose yours this time, there will be another game in need of music coming along in a matter of weeks. Think about games when putting together tracks and loops for wider use. The section on selling your music laid out how a simple riff can become a loop for use on the royalty-free platforms, and games can be an extension of that. Game music composition requires a different approach, as games can be linear and repetitive, requiring a subtly different flavour but essentially the same core music throughout. It may be that a single riff could provide the foundation for ten short pieces of music, varying in tempo to match the more and less frenetic moments in the game. Perhaps a title and close variant as well, to bookend the rest of the pieces. Offered either singly or as a collection, we've found another outlet for music you already have!

You might want to hold back some of your shorter loops from the sharing platforms for the purpose, since game developers are going to want music that is distinctive and could become identifiably 'theirs'. Exclusivity will often be expected, but good payment can be expected in return. It would likely not be of the order you might expect for the life of a royalty-free music library piece over its entire life, but nor is that long-term income guaranteed. This weighing up of options takes experience and ultimately luck - will the long-term income from ongoing downloads of a piece exceed that being offered for a one-time deal? Reference to your wider catalogue may inform that decision to an extent, just as it may strengthen your hand in negotiations around fees. Ultimately though, diversification is really important to make money as a musician today, so if your willingness to take a chance on a lower return to get into the games composition market for the sake of a few seconds of music and potential for a few hundred dollars lost in ongoing revenue, I'd take that in a heartbeat! A few hundred pounds in your pocket right now is never a bad thing, as well as the writing credit for the music, which can go straight up on your website with all the others to help drive more work your way in the future!

Another solid route for game music is the new breed of freelance, or 'gig', Internet sites where people offer various services in return for a fee, music being no exception. Games developers are on these sites advertising their services to develop games for customers to their requirements. Those developers need music, and they're already on the site advertising. It would be very easy for them to browse the site, find your music available, or your composition services to specific requirements available. A fee for a specific piece of music is commissioned composition and becomes another service you can offer. You will also have ample opportunity to refer potential customers to your music library catalogue, potentially feeding downloads there too!

Music Library / Stock Music Composition

The earlier section on selling your music first introduced the concepts of music library, royalty-free and stock music; all of which mean the same thing to you – music sold for a fee, with no ongoing royalty due. As you are writing the music you're recording, it has become another avenue for composition! More or less every video you've ever watched on a video sharing platform has music, and the video sharing sites do not allow the use of copyrighted material without redirecting all advertising revenue to the copyright holder. So everyone who ever shares a video on any subject who wishes to monetise it needs royalty-free music. Surprisingly perhaps, even major studios do not have musicians available for every production, and budgets would not allow it to be otherwise, hence a burgeoning market for music library and stock music. It is also possible to earn a good income by composing and providing tracks to reseller platforms specialising in stock music.

You may have heard of 'stock images'; pictures made available for commercial re-use by their creators for a one-off fee. You could be producing 'stock music' for use in Internet video, TV ads, TV shows, computer games, promotional materials and much more. People looking for royalty-free music to accompany their work are plentiful, and they're looking for just about everything from the simplest drum loop or guitar riff, to full choral pieces, orchestral opuses and everything in between. The larger organisations may have relationships with artists, studios and record companies, and have access to music via various means, though many do not. For mere mortals, or independents just like us, music library Internet sites are often the easiest way to find quality music at affordable prices quickly enough to meet an immediate need.

It is possible to make a very good income from any finished piece of music, regardless of length up to a point. You will find advice in the recording section to get into the habit of recording yourself all the time, even during practice. You may find a melody that once a drum loop and an underlying bass line has been added, would not be out of place as a backing groove for a corporate promo video. And all you had to do was take the thirty-second clip you already had, spend ten minutes editing it, and upload it to the music library site. We should all be big on extracting maximum value from our time and resources - so re-use of material is job number one for all of us.

Instrumental loops can be uploaded with modest variation in tempo, pitch, length and underlying rhythm to create several separate and distinct stock music products for customer download. Full tracks can also be offered for royalty-free download. Some of the stock music sites require exclusivity, whilst others will go as far as commissioning you to create tracks for them to sell to their customers. The best approach is the one that is best for you, personally I diversify and direct my product in all available directions:

★ Exclusivity typically pays most in percentage terms, some up to 65%, but you need to ensure the site you choose can get you the sales. It is best to push 'pop' material in this direction.

★ Upload the bulk of your royalty-free music to sites that do not demand exclusivity. These will pay between 35% and 50% typically, but are likely to see more downloads.

★ Write tracks on commission if the fee offered makes it worthwhile to you. Fees are often in the region of £500 per track, but the tracks need to be professional and generally include vocals. Frankly, such a track is to my mind worth more sold directly from your website and the digital platforms.

Being successful with stock music relies on being as mainstream as possible within your genre, so whilst all the fringes of the industry are represented, the more esoteric your music is, the fewer people it will appeal to and thus the fewer sales you are likely to secure. This is not a world that rewards creative excess; the goal is almost to create as inoffensive a background as possible for a broader piece of work the customer needs a musical contribution for. The music in these settings is typically not centre-stage. With that in mind, if you're going to go this route, compose music specifically for the purpose. You can still come up with a fantastic hard rock riff and back it up with some killer drums, but if you come away from the edit believing you've got something really fantastic you might want to head toward the paid digital download sites, retaining royalties, rather than letting it go for a few pounds or dollars.

Stock music is provided to the customer royalty-free for a one-off cost, and also almost always without attribution, meaning if you take this route you may be unaware where your music has been used and who by. The listener will also be unaware that the music they can hear has been produced by you. The reward for stock music is purely financial at the point of sale - whilst some passive income is possible in terms of a track being downloaded for months to come, delivering a fee each time, no payments are associated with the volume of airplay the completed work receives. If the standard download fee for your track is £34, and your cut is £17, it is £17 you will receive whether your music was used in a home movie that nobody watched, or a cinema trailer for a Hollywood blockbuster. Royalty-free is royalty-free.

It is possible, though not a regular occurrence, for a piece of stock music to hit the big time. Back in 2005, a band called B.E.R were commissioned to write an 80s style rock song for a music library, and 'The Night Begins to Shine' was born. For the next 9 years, not a great deal happened. The song was used, sampled, downloaded and so on by users of the music library until 2014 when a major studio needed a piece of music for a cartoon series. The cartoon episode in question had an 80s sort of a vibe, and the producer of the show, lacking access to live musicians or the budget to engage them, headed for stock music. One search for '80s style rock song' and a few clicks later, B.E.R's music is featuring in a cartoon being shown globally. Moreover, fans of the show enjoyed the song and it became a recurring theme, finally spawning a four cartoon series about the song itself in 2017. That cartoon series took B.E.R to new heights as the song made it to No.26 of the US chart, and was covered by a couple of globally renowned acts for the same series. 12 years after writing, a song went from royalty-free download to a 10-second burst on a cartoon, to the top end of the music charts being covered by big-name artists! Crazy!

Would you have heard of B.E.R were it not for that event? Nor me were it not for my 6-year-old son Alex, who loves that cartoon!

Jingles

Traditionally, jingles were a mega-big business. The big campaigns over the years have created some truly memorable pieces of music now synonymous with the products in question. The prevalence of music in advertising has abated to some extent, with average TV advertisements lasting only 15 seconds, and changes in the way the viewing public consume television; skipping advertising and watching online are the habit of many. It is also increasingly common for advertisers to license records by big-name artists of use in their advertising campaigns. Regardless, the majority of advertisements feature music of some description, even if just a handful of notes accompanying the appearance of the company logo.

Writing jingles is not massively different from the composition of any other form, with the exception that you will generally be working to a quite specific brief as well as to tight timescales. Very often the product company will have commissioned an advertising company to create an ad, and once the advertising company has created the concept, shot the ad and booked the first slot for it to air, they'll remember they don't have any music! Cue panicked telephone calls to music houses, agencies, contacts, and people who know people, in search of someone who can turn around a piece of music to the brief double quick!

The process will start with a request for a piece of music of a particular length, with a customer view on the feel of that piece of music in terms of genre: 'should sound like...' or similar. It may be specific; it may be a vague instruction to be 'not too jazzy...' (which is of course pretty open to interpretation). Sometimes you'll get a rough edit of the ad so you know what you're working with. Sometimes a storyboard (a comic book style frame by frame layout) may be provided. On occasion, neither. The customer wants to hear some music to help shape their artistic vision. Very occasionally there will be lyrics, but this is not typical, owing to the potential for the jingle lyrics and the message of the ad to conflict. You're more likely to have to bring the levels up and down to work with the voiceover track.

The mechanism for the process is similar to being commissioned to write a track for the music libraries. You'll be given a ballpark to work in and a deadline, it may then be in your interests to create a couple of variations on the theme, since the ultimate decision maker will be the company who commissioned the advertising work. It is possible to spend time and effort creating a piece that they are not satisfied with and that doesn't get purchased. Don't panic though, should that come to pass you still have a piece of music that can be used in other avenues - stock music if nothing else.

If your music is selected you can expect a fee to be paid immediately by the commissioning agency, which is typically between five and ten percent of the total budget. This can be anything from a handful of hundreds to a couple of handfuls of thousands, depending on the job in question and your contract with the agency. You will then get royalties from plays of the ad on the air. Make sure you are signed up with the performing rights organisations; the agency should file all the paperwork, but this is your money we're talking about so best for you to make sure they all know you've got a commercial airing. As with the other royalties we have talked about previously, it is unlikely to get beyond a few hundred pounds a month, but all those hundreds add up pretty nicely - passive income from work you completed years ago, and you're still getting paid!

Concert Composers

And finally we get there - the section you probably expected when reading about making a living as a composer. The powdered wig (now optional), grand piano (optional) and a mountain of manuscript paper (which, though virtual, you're probably stuck with). All the available routes for making a living from composition are a tricky proposition, but this has to be the most arduous. You're into the same one in a million shot to stardom territory that would see you topping out the chart, selling out your favourite supersize concert venue every night for a month or having your first ten records all going triple platinum. Because there frankly isn't an enormous market for classical music, there isn't a huge market for classical performers, and they're not looking for new music to play when they're not really playing. Meanwhile, the majority of audiences looking for classical music are after the hits - the Beethoven, Mozart and Brahms numbers we all know, whether we know what they are or not. Maybe a bit of Vivaldi... anyway.

About the only shots you've got here if you will insist on a yesteryear approach to being a composer are:

★ Being commissioned by a theatre to compose the music for a show, or;

★ Reinventing the wheel, whilst adding your unique spin.

The former is pretty self-explanatory, and aligns itself with the path for film. You want to fill the Broadway halls with your music, but you're probably not going to march right in there with a swagger of over-confidence and pull that one off. You're going to want to start with small and local performance groups of more modest means, who will be grateful for your contribution and with a bit of luck pay you a bit for your time and trouble. I've only ever ended up here for a favour, or after a lot of persuading. Usually both. You would not usually find me writing a score for a children's performance at a local drama school, and you'd be even less likely to find me there playing day after day for the rehearsals as well as the performances themselves. I was paid, but not enough to make it worth doing -

I guess my reward for that one was more spiritual than financial. At least the experience made the next step more attainable, in theory at least, since I never took it!

The reinvention thought is essentially to play to your public. If we accept they're looking for more of the music they already know and love, you would be wise from a financial point of view to stick pretty close to the proven formula. I expect this to cause the same injury to artistic sensibilities as the suggestion of forming a covers band to play functions. OK, I guess if you intentionally follow the path cut by the big guys and never deviate from it, maybe you're not really sticking to the purity of your vision. But back in the real world you need to eat, and giving the people what they want has half a chance of satisfying that objective. Once you've got them hooked, there is nothing to stop you risking it all with more of a concept record next time out. You could probably keep the wolf from the door with submissions to music libraries as well. About the only positive I can think of offering you on the classical world in today's market is that there are way fewer people competing in that area than most others, so in terms of raw numbers you're probably better off.

Sorry, I tried, and as a frustrated cellist I wanted to succeed - but I can't make an attempt at making a living from music by being a concert composer feel like a good idea. You probably need to be a star for that one!

Potential Income

Potential income from composing is another area where if you do manage to pull off that one in a million shot, bump into a major league producer in the street while listening to your latest track… and the rest is history, you could be huge! If you manage to channel Beethoven, get the plaudits from a notoriously fickle critical community and start packing out the concert halls (having dusted them off appropriately first), you're going to make a fortune from the shows, as well as the sales of CDs and downloads. Maybe even the odd shirt or hat! Maybe you'll get chatting with a top-ten artist in a bar, who just fancies taking a chance on you, or be watching a film humming a tune unaware that a big-time director is sat right behind you. Maybe; but maybe not.

Freelance composers typically get paid per piece, in the region of five to ten percent of the overall budget, but since that budget could be anything from nothing to six-figures there is no set fee as such. You would do well, as advised elsewhere, to have a minimum hourly rate you are content to accept. Factors such as experience, availability, delivery against a brief and frankly how much they love your work can make a huge impact on the financial result. If your composition features in a national broadcast, your earning potential increases dramatically with royalties for every play to a significant potential audience. A single score for film or a high-profile advertising campaign could pay **£30,000** - and once again we've all but hit the 'success' line in one well-crafted manoeuvre.

Meanwhile, back on planet realistic, the majority of composers would do well to make an adequate living from composition alone and there is no denying it. The field is competitive, and if you're a composer in the truest sense - that you write music for others to perform, it is a difficult trade to break into. It is difficult to provide a solid figure for planning purposes for the simple reason that one amazing result could blow any estimate clean out of the water, but if we focus on the more accessible tangents of mobile game and stock music, income derived from pieces of music suitable for those forums is based to a significant extent on how much you create, which leads fairly directly to how much time you spend doing it.

From my experience of the music library sites, I believe it is realistic to create a couple of tracks per month in amongst various other commitments, which could be tweaked and twisted into half a dozen downloadable items of various lengths. It is then realistic to expect a **£500 per month** income from downloads of those tracks. Going the royalty-free route you forgo any ongoing payments, but that still represents 20% of the income we're looking for as a minimum. Not too shabby at all!

Real world example

I think we can agree that working full-time as a composer and making a sufficient income is unlikely. You would need either one very solid gig, a TV show broadcast nationally, a film or similar big ticket item, or a network of contacts sufficient to provide you with near full-time work. In so doing you would be a professional musician, no doubt about that, but when we set out in search ultimately of freedom, what we would have found would be a full-time job.

Making a good living from composition is not impossible, as there are people who do it. But there are not many people who do it. Trading in a job with a salary for a life of stress as you wait for the next commission is not something I could recommend. That is not to say that composition cannot be a key contributor to your overall offering as a musician. If you are writing your own music, it follows that you could write it for others. It could additionally be argued that all the money you make from sales of your own music is reliant on your skills in composition, and your income would take a significant hit without it. That contribution is captured elsewhere, and cannot be readily separated from the other components of music sales. I keep reminding you how strong a proposition it is to get paid repeatedly for the same slice of your time, and my income contribution from composition is no exception. I have split out my income from royalty-free music into the fixed fee income I received for a specific collection of music, versus that captured below. The £8,000 below is made up of downloads of short loops and fills sold on various sample and music library sites, that by virtue of the length of the pieces in question I consider to be derived from composition. The items are not finished articles, but tools that others can use to finish their projects. By that rationale, I am contributing to other people's music with my own, and that's a modern take on composition. My current income derived from composition is as follows:

Music Library / Stock Music (Annual)	£8,000
Total	**£8,000**
Time Spent (Monthly)	~30hrs

There will be some residual income from traffic to my websites and links to my wider body of work from the music library sites. As I have outlined previously, I continue to split out all my recorded work for listing on the music library and stock music sites, because a successful and significant income from them is based on volume. The more music you have available of good quality, the more you will sell.

The Left Field

Overview

★ ★ ★ ★ ☆ Difficulty

★ ☆ ☆ ☆ ☆ Cost

★ ★ ☆ ☆ ☆ Time Commitment

★ ★ ☆ ☆ ☆ Likelihood of Success

★ ★ ☆ ☆ ☆ Income Potential

Required resources: A willingness to think of making a livelihood in the modern music industry in a broader context. An appreciation for less obvious income possibilities, and maybe an instrument!

It will not have been lost on you that people make money in music with no discernable talent. Specialists in being in the right place at the right time, being willing to wear less than anybody else, say something horrific on social media, do something horrific and become notorious via social media... you know, that whole 'no such thing as bad publicity' thing? Well, it's a way to go for sure, but there are other options to make money on the (perfectly legal!) fringes of the music industry that you might want to consider.

This section cannot be exhaustive because no matter how crazy you and I think something is, you can pretty much guarantee that someone has already been there, seen and done it. There will almost certainly be a t-shirt. But that doesn't mean there isn't room for you too.

To be entirely fair, the concepts in this section aren't crazy at all; they're routes to a meaningful income that may not scream out at you when considering a career in music. Many are not even news - musicians have been working at them for some time, and will doubtless continue to do so in the future. Concerts in retirement homes, running musician's retreats, you could even go all sensible and head to university with a view to becoming a music teacher or music therapist! They're not crazy options at all, but would be a pretty serious undertaking with four years of formal study required. If you're interested though, don't let me put you off - I've done my share of classroom stuff and done very well out of it. I'd recommend a formal music education, but it isn't for everyone, and because of that the opportunities it unlocks are not for this book.

There are several fields of music that barely get any exposure. For instance, when you see a pop starlet on daytime TV not miming very well to a backing track, guess what the guy sat next to her with a guitar is doing? Not playing! But he's not playing pretty well, isn't he? Not just waving his hand up and down, he probably could play that part if he needed to. Yes, he probably could. Yet somebody is knowingly paying him not to. I am unsure whether that's technically session work or being a TV extra, but either way, the dude got paid! And he wouldn't have got that job if he wasn't a competent musician.

The less traditional tangents chosen for this section have been selected from the greater group of less obvious ways to make money as a musician because of their accessibility. They either dovetail with strategies in the rest of this book, fit neatly with strategies already employed by working musicians, or require a minimal investment in time and no financial outlay to set up for an ongoing potential income from future work. Preferably all three.

Extras!

There is good if irregular money to be made just being yourself! Particularly accessible if you live near a big city, filming is happening all the time in locations across the country. The majority of productions require supporting artists, or extras as they are popularly known. It doesn't matter if you're young or old, short or tall, thin or... not, the agencies specialising in these gigs need people of more or less any description. You might even get to rub shoulders with a star or two along the way!

The good news doesn't stop there either. As a musician, if you're occupying the distinctive end of the visual spectrum, as many of us invariably do, you could carve a niche as 'angry looking punk #3', for example. Tattoos and piercings might not get you a job in the local law courts, but having more of a look than the majority of people will get you work. Having a particular set of talents is also a saleable bonus; playing an instrument as well as singing or dancing, could all land you a job one step up from the random background bystander jobs typical for the field.

You don't need any formal acting experience, as my foray into film noir testifies, but you do need to arrive reliably and ideally early, as well as being able to take direction. If you're supposed to be looking wistfully to the left when the camera lands on you, then that is what you need to be doing when the time comes. Supporting artists are typically booked for a day at a time, obviously that 'day' could be an evening or the dead of night depending on the requirements for filming. The job could last several days, again based on the schedule.

Getting yourself into position for this kind of work is easy enough: simply register with casting agencies specialising in film extras. It will be easy to find a number of options in your geographical area via your favourite search engine. Make sure to look for those recognised by Equity, and be wary of anyone asking for payment in return for photography up front; typically their business model is exactly that, charging for pictures that do not lead to work. If in doubt, search out online reviews of the casting company online. Agents should not charge any fees to sign up, with fees typically recovered from your first paying job. That gives them appropriate incentive to offer you work! From there on, something in the region of 15% of your daily fee goes to the casting agent.

There are several advantages to signing up with an agency in readiness for film work. Firstly, there is a lot of work out there, and if you are flexible and available you can position yourself well for any opportunity for someone with your basic physical makeup. The work is sporadic, which although a disadvantage from the point of view of economic certainty, I prefer to see as a positive since the income is a nice boost without requiring a massive commitment in time. The money is good, with fees of around £100 per day the going rate, with the possibility of an uplift if you get more time on camera, interaction with the main cast or a couple of lines of dialogue. Someone needs casting as the house band in the dive bar scene, and who better than the musician who already looks like a musician and can do a convincing job of it?

On to the downsides, which really are limited to the irregular availability of work. You might be busy for four days in a week, then not get any work for a couple of weeks. When work comes you are obviously free to decline it based on your wider schedule, but be aware that agents, like everybody else, appreciate reliability. Turn down work too often and you may find the offers stop coming. Work as an extra is not to be relied upon as a primary source of income, but it is surprisingly available as a top up to your other revenue streams. On that basis it is definitely worthy of consideration, and at least you're getting yourself into show business!

House Concerts

House concerts are private events in people's homes, with friends and neighbours of the host making up the guest list. A relatively new phenomenon in the UK, and still not widely known, the house concert has been a staple for the touring musician in the US for some years - providing pit stops along the way, as well as a much-needed boost to income.

The basic mechanics are straightforward: the host seeks to put on a house concert, and a fee will be agreed with the artist. The host will then send invites out to their friends and acquaintances, as well as the artist's mailing list or social media group by agreement, then seek donations from those accepting the invitation. The donations are generally paid in advance to guarantee that costs are covered. The hosts then open up their home to the performer and the audience, with food and drink provided by the host and/or by those in attendance, depending on the preferences of the individual host.

If you're not a big name artist, you're going to want to work some crowd pleasers into your set for such events. A few well-placed covers will go down well, especially if the arrangement is interesting and unmistakably 'you'. Playing people's homes is plainly a different experience to a more traditional concert venue. The audience is likely to be less than five feet away, and you're going to need an 'unplugged' kind of a setup to be successful - you don't want a full drum kit, Marshall stack, and piano in somebody's living room. The intimacy of such settings emphasises the often repeated importance of likeability. You're not expected to roll up for a house concert with your rock star attitude, play and leave. Your host is going to expect you to be engaged and engaging, as well as putting in a solid performance. You are a guest as well as a performer in this setting, so you need to be comfortable making friends in perpetually new crowds.

In terms of income potential, it is sensible to request a guaranteed minimum. You would not want to travel to somebody's home to find an embarrassed host explaining that nobody is coming. It is possible for everyone to win from this setup. Requesting a £300 minimum for a house concert means that a host only need recover £12 from 25 people to get a free concert in their home. Were this set of circumstances to pass, the host gets a free concert, you get a decent payday as well as very likely dinner and a pleasant evening, and the guests get a more intimate and immersive musical experience than they will with £12 anywhere else. Fantastic. Remember as well that although your audience is smaller, they are likely to be much more engaged than a general concert audience, making your chances of shifting some CDs a great deal better than average!

As ever, listing house concerts on your website along with video clips that showcase your playing to smaller audiences will be extremely helpful, along with a repertoire so people know what to expect. You can also take requests in advance to ensure you deliver the performance your audience wants to see and hear, making sure the experience is as good as it can be. As with so many aspects of professional music, a number of directories have appeared online in recent years that put hosts and performers together, assisting in the negotiations around fees and scheduling, as well as providing a marketplace for the transaction and even organising tickets if necessary. These can be very helpful to people who are welcoming unknown performers into their homes, and can drastically improve your success rate beyond your immediate circle. They will, of course, take a fee, some from the host, some from the performer, and some via surcharges on tickets.

Online Concerts

As an extension of the house concert performance concept, technology has made it possible for musicians to go to their audience, rather than the audience coming to them. Where is your audience right now? Probably at home, and almost certainly within the range of an Internet-connected device.

And presto! High speed and stable Internet connections, as well as low-cost computer and audio equipment have made it possible to stream performances around the world at a moment's notice. It is very simple to use any of the social media platforms to stream video in real time, use technology built into smartphones to establish a video connection to an individual or group, and set yourself up for a virtual concert right now! How else would you be able to connect with a global fan base simultaneously for almost no overhead?

Musicians today are making money doing exactly this. They might be providing personalised performances for individuals or small groups with personalised birthday and seasonal greetings proving to be popular sales for musicians. Offering live performances by way of competition prizes is also popular in return for wider exposure via social media. Most exciting perhaps are the online platforms that allow musicians to stream concerts to a worldwide audience. Tickets are sold for the event, and the musician can even specify how many tickets must be sold before he or she will commit to scheduling the concert. Reaching a global audience has never been easier; you could schedule a concert for next week, publicise via social media and be performing in seven days without the logistical difficulties of venue, transport, shipping equipment and everything else. The online platforms, available as ever via your chosen search engine, have evolved to the point that they are publicity vehicles themselves; keeping diaries of upcoming online events to share with thousands of users worldwide. As ever, they take their cut, but since the musician has barely had to do any work to arrange a concert and can pretty much turn up and play, that seems only fair. The service includes the systems required to stream your concert as well; you only need a mechanism to get the material to them, and they do the rest.

Typically, the online platforms take around 50% of the fees gathered from the viewing public. That might seem punitively high, with the artist providing the entertainment, but without the platform there would be no show, and it does mean the musician can operate with zero overheads. The ability to specify the number of tickets that must be sold before the concert is scheduled also makes it possible to guarantee a minimum income for the show, placing all the control in the hands of the artist. With that in mind, it would be theoretically possible to make a huge income from a single show, given that the performer could simply wait until the millionth ticket was sold - whether that would happen before those already committed lost interest is another question. A commitment to host such a concert within three months of publicising the possibility seems reasonable, so it is a question for the individual how many fans can be mobilised by word of mouth, social media and other existing groups such as mailing lists, and the online streaming platforms themselves. An income equivalent to a house concert is a sensible minimum expectation and is very likely to mean you only need a hundred people to commit. The show is recorded by the streaming provider and retained for future use as well, giving the potential for an ongoing income. If you make a habit of such things you may find a viewer of this week's concert enjoys himself so much he reviews your back catalogue and watches a couple more!

The online concert platforms enable and actively promote tipping in addition to ticket sales, providing another opportunity to increase income. So you're looking at an online venue where you can put on a show for nothing and busk at the same time. Links to your website and digital downloads should go without saying by now. And I used to drive myself to bars, be my own roadie, play, clear everything away and drive home for fifty quid! What was I thinking?

Gear Rental

Another basic concept evolved in today's interconnected world. Lending your stuff to people isn't a particularly revolutionary concept. We've all been there; guitar volume pots become scratchy as hell, a keyboard that mysteriously stops working or an amp with no output. Maybe your guitar has turned up in Rio when the rest of your gear, and you, have just arrived in Prague. My favourite to date? The power supply for my whole pedal board deciding to give up on me, leaving me with next to nothing - and all these things are, by whatever law that creates such inevitable stress and unhappiness, always destined to happen within striking distance of a gig, studio session or similar make or break moment.

Cue pleas to social media, followed by hurried calls to friends, relatives and local stores looking for the item you need. Then pretty smartly on to calls to people who barely know people that you know through someone else, in an increasingly desperate search for that elusive piece of the sonic puzzle you simply cannot be without. With a bit of luck, you'll find something sort of like what you were looking for. Note to self to always buy a backup!

No more! Well, that whole fun game still exists and remains as difficult to play as ever, but thanks to the social media-centric world of today, life has gotten dramatically easier. It is now possible to find musical equipment of all flavours via online marketplaces. From a 60's Fender Twin or vintage Gibson Les Paul to give you that authentic rock and roll presence, to a set of maracas for that final piece of stage flourish, they've got you covered. Listings are popping up for all sorts of items, in every conceivable geographical location. And guess what? If people need to rent gear for performance or recording in a hurry, you can make money making it available for rent!

Simply provide a breakdown of your inventory on the site: item type, model, condition and the amount you want to receive in rental (usually 10% of its value per day), and you're good to go. Photographs of the gear may help grease the wheels and encourage people in search of that elusive item. Your address is only shared with the rental community once a transaction has been agreed, so no security concerns there, and this could be a great way to make a bit of money here and there for the effort it took to list the item. There is no fee; the sites charge the rental customer a premium on top of the figure you state as your minimum rental payment. Unless your collection is really extensive, a one-off exercise of an hour or so could see your whole collection available for rent, though obviously nobody would recommend making your pride and joy or 'go to' instruments available for rental. Everything is insured, ensuring damage is paid for, and security deposits are taken to cater for anything up to the full value of the item to be charged to the renter. But plainly, accidents happen and fixing the damage cannot fully fix the problem for an item you truly care about.

You are not obliged to rent out your gear even once listed on the marketplace - if you don't get a good vibe from the person looking to rent, don't agree to it. Ask what the plan is for your gear, and if you're not happy with your pristine vintage saxophone being used for a month-long tour of back-alley dive bars across the continent, just say "no thanks".

Gear rental is a great way to make a little extra money. Sure, it's a bit hit and miss and the income is reliant on someone looking for exactly what you've got available, but it costs nothing to list your gear, takes very little time and provides an opportunity to make money from equipment that would otherwise just be sat around gathering dust. What's not to like?

Selling Gear

Don't panic! I'm not going to tell you to sell your gear. In fact, I really wouldn't suggest you ever sell your gear unless you're really sure the replacement is an upgrade. Certainly, if you're attempting to make money from music, selling the tools of your trade would be counter-productive. If you're really stuck, at least trade in your USA Fender Stratocaster for a second-hand Affinity from an auction site

- don't leave yourself with nothing! I sold a Gibson SG twenty years ago because I felt I needed a beer fund more than that guitar. That and the terrible Hamer guitar I replaced it with haunt me to this day!

But that isn't really what this section is about. If you've been playing a while, you'll be able to appreciate different instruments. If you've been buying them for a while and keeping an eye on social media music groups for idle interest and impulse buys (G.A.S - Guitar Acquisition Syndrome. Look it up, it's real!), you'll know what the going rate for a '91 Charvel Fusion is. And if you have a little cash available, you can use your knowledge and experience to make money buying and selling gear. You can also use your musicianship to enhance your service and boost your sales.

The key to making money from selling gear is buying at the right price. Internet auction sites represent a fantastic opportunity for bargain hunting, bringing a world of items for sale to your fingertips. There are several factors that make Internet auction sites fantastic places to buy at the right price:

★ An auction listing may have been badly created, resulting in little interest. Typos and listing completely the wrong item are not at all uncommon.

★ An auction listing may say 'Charvel Guitar', creating little interest, but you know the pictures show a Model 6, worth way more than the seller is asking.

★ Items listed without reserve can go for next to nothing, and you could get a real result.

★ The pictures will, probably without exception, be terrible.

★ You can establish whether you are looking at a bargain guitar easily from the range of prices displayed. If you search for 'Ibanez RG550' and find the top end is a couple of hundred pounds more than the item you're thinking of buying, you know the item is well within its money.

It is important to check the condition of the item. In some cases, minor damage can be seen as a badge of honour and a working instrument may well have seen modest cosmetic wear. If you are dealing with instruments that are decades old, it becomes increasingly unlikely that they've remained pristine. These days, guitar manufacturers actually charge more to take a new guitar from the factory and beat it tastefully to mimic a lifetime of heavy gigging! But there are some instances where that damage completely devalues the piece. A '59 Les Paul might sell for a quarter of a million, but a '59 Les Paul that has taken a tumble out of the back of a truck is worth very little. Neck breaks on guitars are a fantastic example of this - if repaired correctly the break might be almost invisible and the glue is almost certainly stronger than the wood, but the more you have to explain that to a potential buyer the less likely the sale becomes, and the less you'll be able to realise from the sale. Make sure you carefully review the photographs of an item and don't be afraid to ask the seller questions as well as asking for more pictures if there is anything you're unsure of.

Next up, make sure you set yourself a limit on an auction and do not exceed it in the heat of battle. All the action on the online auctions happens within minutes (usually seconds) of the end of the listing, and what looked like a steal three days ago can rocket up in price pretty quickly. The temptation to get dragged along with the competition for just one more bid is very strong, and I've fallen for it myself, but you need to have a clear idea in your mind of what the item is worth, and make sure there is enough of a margin between the sale price and that you hope to realise. Guitar shops typically double their money on sales - I'm usually happy with 20%. Keeping in mind that 20% is probably best case, and 10% isn't a bad place to end up.

Pawn shops are also good places to score a bargain for three pretty straightforward reasons:

★ That the person selling initially needed the money in a hurry, so the pawn shop paid very little for the item and that means they do not need to realise its full value to make their money.

★ The pawn shop may not know what the item is, and hence what it is actually worth. This used to be a massive advantage to the knowledgeable buyer but is one of few areas of life the Internet has made worse. Now anyone can type a vague description and a serial number into a search engine and find out exactly what they're looking at. Sigh.

★ The pawn shop will do less trade in higher value items, making it very likely that a guitar with a £500 ticket on it can be negotiated downward pretty easily and substantially.

So, let's assume you've scored your bargain. Once you have it in your hands you will be able to add value very quickly by giving the item a good clean and polish and taking some decent pictures of it. Not the badly lit, propped up in the corner by the coats pictures like those that accompanied the online auction. Think about how you present the item. A very easy way to get a good quality result is to position the item on your bed with a plain cover and take pictures from above - if done from appropriate range it will not be obvious the background is a bed. Take pictures from all angles, including detailed close-ups of any war wounds/blemishes or other areas of interest. Put yourself in the place of the buyer and think about what you'd want to see, and make sure that is what you give them. What questions would you ask? Answer them.

You can really add value as a musician though. Selling an item from a knowledgeable position makes you a compelling proposition as a salesperson, but you have to be completely honest in your appraisals of instruments. I have sold instruments very successfully online alongside other ventures for several years. My unique selling point? Every guitar I list for sale is accurately described in detail with at least ten high-quality pictures, and most importantly a video of me playing it in demonstration. If people are going to be buying without laying their hands on an item, being able to see it in action is extremely helpful and reassuring to them, as it would be to you or I. I also gather a little bit of extra income from the advertising positioned on the video hosted by the sharing platforms for each view. The video is also posted to social media as a sales tool, generating yet more video traffic and advertising revenue. Multiple income streams for a single effort once again. And all I was doing was videoing myself practicing for less than a minute with each guitar - a minimal overhead.

Your own website for sales gives the best return - I have a site dedicated to instrument sales and an associated group on social media with a few thousand members. Selling through that medium allows me to retain all income, where auction sites take a significant commission. You may find, as I did, that once you're established people are willing to pay direct rather than via online payment companies, who again take a percentage from the transaction. The same online auction site you bought your item from can bring you the sale, and if the item is correctly presented with good quality pictures, you can expect to realise an additional 20%. With fees taken into account though you may find your margin reduced to 9% - not as healthy but still potentially helpful as a contribution to wider income. The auction sites are very good for exposure, but with luck potential customers will find your website and buy direct; perhaps not to start with but once you start building your reputation. As with everything else in life, relationships are everything.

My core value is that of being a musician first and of genuinely loving to play and selling instruments I'd very happily keep myself. To that end, my standing offer is to take back any instrument I have sold, no questions asked. I have yet to have a single instrument returned, or anything but contentment and appreciation from my customers. Each year I buy and sell approximately thirty guitars. The average margin (the difference between buy and sell) is thirty percent, meaning I make approximately £4,000 per year. Between buying, listing for sale with pictures and video, packaging, and shipping, I would estimate two hours of effort per guitar or five hours per month on average. I also save a related amount on buying guitars, since I can effectively have them on loan for a period before moving them on.

I'll confess I'm imperfect though, there are several that never got sold, and I probably haven't tried very hard to help them along!

Crowdfunding

Included as a modern-day concept; a funding mechanism rather than a paying job, crowdfunding is the process by which you state your intentions and a monetary target, willing participants pay amounts of money in return for specified items or services, and the project commences once the funding target has been reached. The leading player in the crowdfunding market reports over £100m ($120m) has been received by successful music projects, some twenty thousand projects run by artists to fund album production. Sums range from a few hundred pounds to over a million for a single project! Some crowdfunding platforms permit artists to retain funding received even if the project does not go ahead. Clearly wealthy friends, a solid following, some sort of hype or notoriety or a very persuasive pitch are required to secure meaningful funding for an album, but crowdfunding can be a great means for independent musicians to fund a tour or a studio project without the backing of a label.

Whilst traditional crowdfunding sees funding requests for specific enterprises, some of the newer twists on the theme encourage ongoing patronage. Rather than seeking funding for the production of a music video in return for advance copies, merch, executive producer credits and the like, the new model embraced by online platforms sees fans committing ongoing support for an artist and agreeing to pay a specified amount for each piece of content that is released. The leading player in this space reports seven figure pay-outs every month to their artists by seeking ongoing support from their fan base. This could be a very persuasive proposition for musicians with an active following on social media and solid participation within their group.

That concept is taken further still by pledge processing companies, who allow fans to pre-order a copy of an album yet to be created and who are in return invited to the inner circle of the production itself. Big bands and solo artists are getting increasingly involved with this movement, and many live stream the recording sessions to the fans supporting them. The average pledge amounts to the equivalent price of four music CDs, with the online platform taking a percentage by way of fees. Many musicians participate in this without the funding component, solely to improve engagement with their fans via dialogue and social media.

Overall, crowdfunding can be a fantastic mechanism to fund the production of an album or a tour by what amounts to advance sales. It has the added benefit of driving engagement with fans and starting to build hype in advance. Those fans have the potential to act as ambassadors for your brand, putting out the good work and increasing your exposure to a wider audience. It may seem alien to you to ask for money for what is, at this stage anyway, nothing. Most of us feel the same, but there is a profound truth to the statement that if you don't ask, you won't get.

Potential Income

Potential income from all the jobs on the side you could fit around the edges of your core business is limited only by your willingness to do it! I have chosen examples of which I have direct experience, and as I'm a fairly standard sort of a guy, I have to assume my experience is in line with an average one.

The potential for success here is huge since there is no end to the possibilities. Maybe you'll get chatting with [insert Hollywood A-lister here] during a gig as a supporting artist, and end up married with kids living the dream. Perhaps you'll find a genuine '59 Les Paul advertised as an Epiphone on an auction site, and pay off your mortgage the following week. I can tell you that all of the examples provided have provided me with a monthly income significant enough to be worthwhile, and play their part alongside my wider work to keep my family and I in the style to which we have become accustomed. It is probably truer to say that the extra income provided by these peripheral activities gives us the opportunity for occasional luxuries, paying for treats and things we didn't need to live, but that made life more fun.

The income from instrument sales requires a financial investment, albeit one that is cyclical - sell an instrument, buy another with half the money, sell that to buy another with half that money and so on. Reserves will creep up gradually. Rental can be a fickle business - my gear may be fashionable or in demand this month, but not next. But it is money for nothing. Work as an extra is a lot more available than you might imagine, and it is worth signing up, but you can find yourself needing to travel to who knows where who knows when. The money is decent for a day's work and again, it costs nothing to make yourself available and see if the phone rings. House concerts are achievable either for musicians in demand or those registered with online companies promoting the events, with online concerts similar. Personal experience says a gig of one flavour or the other might reasonably be expected every couple of months.

These fringe activities should not be considered reliable, but instrument sales are reasonably consistent as a source of income provided you buy well, and rental is available if you possess good quality musical equipment in working order. It is worthwhile registering with the respective agents and organisations specialising in casting supporting artists for film and TV, and house concert promoters, without too great an expectation of success. Better to be pleasantly surprised!

Real world example

My efforts selling musical instruments have proven modestly successful as a side-income, and have brought me on average £4,000 per year - reasonably evenly distributed across the year owing to sales income being reinvested. I also firmly believe I have saved money owing to an ability to feed my guitar habit with instruments I will subsequently sell. I have two electric guitars listed with a popular rental site for a required rental fee of £100 per day, and received a request for a three-week rental of one item, accepting £1,200 for that period.

My work as a film-noir detective was utterly a result of luck; I was already working with the production team on music and was nothing more than about the right physical form for the role, with an ability to walk down a flight of stairs and sit at a desk. Praise indeed.

It happened some years ago, so I will not include the income in the example that follows, but I was paid £400 for three days' work. It was more like an hour of work spread over the course of three days, with a great deal of time getting into costume and being generally prepared, plus a lot of waiting around. It is also only fair to note that despite my portrayal of a gritty PI who men want to be and women want to be with, Hollywood has yet to come calling.

I have had one booking for a house concert in the past year, hosted by a friend of a friend and reasonably well attended, but that says more about the host than my ability to pull a crowd. I'm not a particularly compelling a proposition as a solo act with the whole 'not being a star' thing I have going on. The audience was very generous though, and the tips were greatly appreciated, thank you! I have also hosted a couple of online concerts for small groups, managing to monetise the subsequent recordings with advertising and paid downloads. Back to multiple revenue streams from a single artefact again.

Instrument Sales (Annual)	£4,000
Instrument Rental (Annual)	£1,200
House/Online Concerts (Annual)	£1,800
Total	**£7,000**
Time Spent (Monthly)	~9hrs

There will be some ongoing passive income from downloads of online concert footage, and some advantage to the social media connections I have as a result of instrument sales. In addition to the sales revenue, I have access to 2,500 people via social media who are well engaged, interested in what I do and frequent visitors to the monetised video I use to support sales.

A Month in My Life

In an attempt to help the varied nature of a modern musician's income make sense, I thought it would be helpful to give you a breakdown of a typical month in my life as a musician. Using what I do, when I do it and where the money comes from to provide an insight, I am going to demonstrate how variable work can be, as well as how much freedom there is around my commitments to either take on more work or just enjoy life a bit.

I've had to take a bit of artistic license owing to natural fluctuations in work, but my income is actually reasonably consistent throughout the year. I tend to find that the summer months are busier for weddings whereas spring is bigger for corporate functions. Winter is going to work best for online concerts and in autumn everyone wants to sell their instruments to raise money for the holidays; you're going to make your money there by spending it wisely first. So I've taken what I do in a year and constructed an 'average', though if you pursue a career in music, there is no such thing!

I try to arrange my schedule in two-week cycles: alternating a busy week with a less busy one. Obviously, if work timing is non-negotiable I'll end up with busy weeks back to back rather than turning work down. For the purposes of the example, only two weeks are listed to give an idea of what my working time looks like. A full breakdown of income follows:

Week 1

Monday:

Recording: Studio Day. Up at 6:45am, and on a train to London. In the studio for 8:30, coffee in hand. Working from just after 9am until after 6pm - though only around 3 hours is work, the rest more socialising, relationship building and planning subsequent work. Take advantage of walking past a couple of second-hand shops to check for any new instruments for sale. Home for around 9pm. **14hrs**

Tuesday:

Instrument Sales: Searching Internet auction sites for the type of instruments I typically buy. Note auction end times and set maximum bids. **30mins**

Recording: Home. Retiring to the back-bedroom to see what inspiration comes today. Hit record and start playing for an hour or so, then review the recorded material. Find a few riffs that merit development, isolate and add some virtual instruments. Break for a late lunch and then work on current full track in progress. **8hrs**

Wednesday:

Teaching: Starts with a play through of a popular track with a simplified arrangement. Then building lead technique and demonstrating specific runs and patterns. **1hr**

Recording: Home. Working on partially completed material, evolving, tidying and enhancing. All computer-based work with several variations developed. **4hrs**

Thursday:

Teaching: Beginner lesson. Basic chords and simple songs. **1hr**

Recording: Home. Re-editing existing material to create additional variations with changes to pitch, length and tempo. Tracks completed and uploaded to the stock / royalty-free sites. **3hrs**

Friday:

Teaching: Exam Prep: scales, chords, rhythm & music theory. **1hr**

Production: Some sequencing work in Logic on material from a local band, referred by the bassist in one of my old bands. 3 tracks completed and complemented by virtual instruments. Elements of networking and advice on online marketing offered - all part of the service! **3hrs**

Saturday:

Instrument Sales: Finalise bidding on an Internet auction item and arrange shipping. **30mins**

Performance: Wedding reception for some friends of friends. Two forty-five minute sets, some stock repertoire, some classical arrangements of pop numbers and occasional requests. Sold a couple of CDs, though I assume to the drunkest people in the room! **3hrs**

Sunday:

Website Updates: Uploading new material to my website, checking advertising revenues and click throughs. Change a couple of banners by way of experiment and add a blog entry to give anyone interested enough to read it an update on the coming week. **2hrs**

Total Hours: 41hrs

Email & Social Media: Keeping up with various communications. Late evening on my laptop whilst sat in front of the TV. **30mins each day**

Week 2

Monday:

Recording: Home. Re-editing existing material to create additional variations with changes to pitch, length and tempo. Tracks completed and uploaded to the stock / royalty-free sites. **3hrs**

Tuesday:

Instrument Sales: Auction item received. Clean for sale and take photos. Record, edit and upload a demo video and list item on my website. **1hr**

Recording: Home. As always, hit record and start playing for an hour or so, then review the recorded material. Find a few riffs that are worth working on further, isolate them and add some virtual instruments. Break for lunch and then work on current full track in progress. **8hrs**

Wednesday:

Teaching: Starts with a play through of a popular track with a simplified arrangement. Then building lead technique and demonstrating specific runs and patterns. **1hr**

Recording: Home. Working on partially completed material by evolving, tidying and enhancing. All computer-based work with several variations developed. **4hrs**

Thursday:

Teaching: Beginner lesson. Basic chords and simple songs. **1hr**

Performance: Dep rock guitar for a local venue. 1hr practice/rehearsal late afternoon. Use opportunity for food to network with the bands and their management. Schmooze, hand out cards, relax backstage then play for around 45 minutes. **5hrs**

Friday:

Teaching: Exam Prep: scales, chords, rhythm & music theory. **1hr**

Production: Finishing material for the band. The remainder of the EP completed and complemented by virtual instruments. More advice on online marketing and social media offered - all part of the service! **3hrs**

Saturday:

Instrument Sales: Package up any instruments sold, remove from the website and arrange shipping. **30mins**

Sunday:

Website Updates: Uploading new material to my website, checking advertising revenues and click throughs. Change a couple of banners by way of experiment and add a blog entry to give anyone interested enough to read it an update on the coming week. **2hrs**

Total Hours: 29.5hrs

Email & Social Media: keeping up with various communications. Late evening on my laptop whilst sat in front of the TV. **1hr each day**

Monthly Income

Online Advertising (Website & Video):	£850
Teaching:	£560
Writing (Articles & Books):	£650
Performing:	£820
Recording:	£1,650
Music Sales::	£1,500
Composition & Royalty-free:	£670
Instrument Sales:	£583
TOTAL:	**£7,283**

Friday has become my 'easy day' over the years. It was the first working day I dropped when making the transition, and I've become quite protective of it ever since. I intentionally try to work my schedule to keep three easier days in succession, since I no longer have weekends fully away from work as I did whilst an employee. Being a musician is, for me, a 7 day a week job. It isn't full-time, but a lot of work goes on here and there through the week - often unplanned but always productive.

I am always working on my own projects, which right now are two Internet blogs on matters music, both of which run advertising and will eventually (hopefully!) bring an income, and a series of books. Being obsessed with understanding everything, I have learned how to put together websites, how to design book covers and so many other things. It all takes time, and I probably don't get as much sleep as I should. That might be my biggest piece of advice to you: do not work all night, you're not really getting ahead. If one of you could take the time to tell me that, I probably won't listen, but it would be appreciated just the same!

You

If you can bounce straight from either a salaried job or a very part-time music career, to a schedule like mine, you're probably doing very well indeed and can skip this section. If my schedule looks ridiculous compared to your reality, and you don't think there is any way in hell you could do that, read on.

I didn't arrive at a full working week as a musician overnight; the transition was gradual. My approach to full-time musicianship has the advantage that the first elements I suggest you embrace can be undertaken at whatever time works for you. Mornings, evenings, lunch breaks and weekends - any free time can be used to start building your new career in music. You can start right now, whether in work or not, and provided you are willing to put the time in, you will get the results. Will it be hard work? Yes, for sure. Anything worth having takes a ton of work. Is it worth it? You tell me - what would you be willing to do to make a living from your talent? To be self-sufficient and never need to defer to anyone else ever again? Well, here's your chance.

First up, get your website done today. No excuses, no putting it off until tomorrow; register a name right now. Once you have done that, most registrars will create you a basic site for a small fee - if you are not in a position to learn how to do it yourself (which doesn't take long at all), take them up on this offer. Once the frame is set up it will be as easy to drive as a word processing package. Everything else you do will hinge on this website, and you will have the ability to turn one piece of work into multiple revenue streams, but you need that website. Sign up for social media accounts as well, and make sure you use all the communication channels regularly. Your favourite search engine can explain how to get the channels automatically feeding each other to save you repeating work.

At roughly the same time, start advertising as a tutor. Put the word out - every time an opportunity arises. Business cards are a great idea, and available very economically via Internet printing companies. Print up some basic flyers using your computer if you can't stretch to paying printing costs right now. Your name, the fact you're a music tutor and some contact details are all you need. A chance conversation could make you £30 an hour with a single student taking a weekly lesson being worth around £1,500 a year to you. Quick mental arithmetic says twenty students would meet our criteria for a successful career as a musician, and a sufficient income, and in twenty hours a week. That's a lot of time free to progress your other aspirations. There are online directories for music tutors. If they're free, sign up immediately. You can schedule lessons on evenings and weekends around existing work commitments until such time as you've got enough money coming in to review your day-job.

You can also schedule writing around your existing schedule. Add the results to your website to help maintain interest and tell the world about yourself. In the fullness of time, you can get some advertising going as well. Approach music websites, especially those on which you are already active, and enquire around opportunities for freelance writing using the examples you have produced to support your pitch. You will be successful eventually and likely sooner rather than later. When you are, that's another monthly income, as well as material for your website and portfolio. Writing has the potential to provide an income from the articles, another from advertising on websites displaying the articles, and the non-financial benefit of a richer portfolio of work - all from one activity!

Record everything, always. Practice plugged into your recording equipment and review the results frequently. In doing so, you can turn practice into potential income. Start developing ideas into sound clips of various lengths, and when you hit upon something catchy make it ready for the stock music sites with virtual instrument tracks - drums and bass are a good start. Consider maximising appeal by creating several versions with different tempos and drum tracks. Register with the stock music sites and upload your tracks, as well as uploading them to your website as examples of your work. Creating a body of work is key for any musician, and on top of that you'll have an income from the stock music download sites and more material on your website.

As an extension to the 'record everything' plan, you might consider video of your playing or editing tracks together. Those videos, once shared online, can again be monetised with advertising as well as being backed by your own music, properly credited for greater exposure. And for work you were doing anyway, just hit the record button and spend a few minutes on the edit and upload.

Performance can be daunting if you're not already doing it, but as a capable musician you owe it to yourself to share your work with an audience. My first experience of playing in public and being paid was busking. A gentle start is available by just sitting on a bench somewhere with a bit of passing foot-traffic, and starting playing. At this point, you're just choosing to play outside, no fuss. Once you've realised you've been doing it for fifteen minutes, a couple of people have smiled as they walked by and nobody has pelted you with rotten fruit, lay your open instrument case on the floor and throw a few coins in. Now carry on playing as you were before and see what happens. Worst case scenario here is you've just gotten over any anxiety you had of this experience, and got some practice in. You might even have managed it in your lunch break from work - points from me for two wins for a single event! Best case scenario is making enough money to pay for lunch.

If you are confident in performance already, work on publicising yourself and your band (if you have one) via the various online directories available for musicians focussed on functions - weddings and corporate are easy to find. Record a few pieces and upload them to your website and write a biography or 'about me' section, add a few pictures and you're done. If work comes, worry about how to schedule it once it is a problem you have to worry about. You could always book a day off work to get paid £200 playing a wedding instead.

Buying and selling instruments online is also very achievable whilst working a day job. Try bidding on auctions during breaks, maybe you can get parcels delivered to work and if not, you can collect them afterwards. Clean up and list for sale on the evenings, using nothing more than the auction site you purchased from if you prefer. Ideally, record a demo video you can monetise for a few extra pennies here and there. Once they sell, package up and ship off during your downtime as well. That alone could bring several hundred pounds a month in for very modest effort.

A combination of the above got me out of full-time work and heading toward musicianship, one day at a time. Many of the activities that will bring you an income in time could be things you are already doing, but now you're taking every available opportunity to monetise them. Even with a full-time job you very likely have at least four usable hours every day and a full weekend in which you can start working on a career in music. Short term toil for a better life felt like a fantastic investment to me, and I hope reading this book has helped to show how achievable a good income from music is to everyone. With hard work and the determination to succeed, you can do exactly what I did.

Make Money in Music Without Being a Star!

In closing

hope you have found this book illuminating and entertaining, and I hope if you were disappointed to be reminded how unlikely global super-stardom is I will have picked you back up with all the information on how you can make money in music without being a star, just like I have. You can make a living and support your family with music, without being a star. That is exactly what the majority of musicians are doing right now; you just don't hear much about them.

However, if money matters start getting a bit tense you should never be too proud to take other work. We all have periods where unexpected expenses come - maybe your car breaks down and is beyond repair. A few shifts here or there as needed are exactly what you should be doing, and the flexible nature of work in music makes it easy to fit other work in around existing commitments, as well as having control of the timings of some other work. You will be able to make it all work, just as I have in the past.

It is for that reason, as well as for good karma, that you should never burn any bridges. Always conduct yourself honestly and with integrity. You might hate your job, your boss might be a nightmare, and you might want with every fibre of your being to tell them exactly where they can shove their job. But even when the time comes for you to quit, don't do it like that. It will bring you minutes of smug satisfaction followed by probable regret. Especially if you need a few hours work here and there, and the employer you just questioned the parentage of would have been in a position to get you out of a jam!

I should also warn you if you haven't already figured it out, that being a musician is not a 9-5 kind of a job. Being self-employed, as you will inevitably be, is not a 9-5 job. It is not an 'easy option', so being a stereotypically lazy and half asleep/drunk musician is not going to produce any results worth shouting about. If you are making the transition from the world of salaried work to making your living as a musician, you are going to have to work harder in the short term. You're probably going to have to work quite a lot harder in the short term. I certainly did. As I recall there were a couple of months when I was starting out where I'd get up at 6:30am, work until 5:30pm (including the commute), and then after eating and spending time with the family I would be working on 'music stuff' until around about midnight every night. Every now and again I'd fall asleep on a Sunday afternoon having not planned to, my batteries being fully depleted. My wife would tell me I worked too hard, I'd grunt and carry on working too hard. I still do that sometimes when I get obsessed with finishing one of my projects.

It gets easier though. The freedom that solid and independent earning potential brings is an incredible feeling. Reliance on your own skills and experience, and talent, is scary at first - can you do it? Will anyone pay you to do it? What about next month? And there will probably be moments like that forever more. But you will also turn your back on the world where an employer can put his hand on your shoulder, tell you how sorry he is, but that he's going to have to let you go. Relying on yourself cannot possibly be any riskier than placing your future in the hands of someone else.

I have no idea how well you're doing right now, but I do know that before I started working as a musician, and formed my own company as a vehicle to achieve it, I was living month to month. It scares me to the core now as I look back, but I pretty much got paid, burned it all over the course of the month and was starting to get a bit twitchy by pay day. I didn't think about it at the time, which is I assume how the world keeps turning and the majority of people avoid nervous breakdowns, but what would happen if you lost your job today? Could you pay the mortgage next month? What about the month after that? I'm betting almost everybody reading this would be in big trouble by month three. But if you start working for yourself, you will never to worry about being unemployed again!

Sure, you might find there are times where money is a bit tight or work not as plentiful as you'd like, and that is why it is so important to diversify. Perhaps you made good money with your first record, but the second one tanked - and there goes a huge chunk of music sales revenue that might have accounted for 20% of your income last year. Teaching and writing are always good safety nets, with more and more people wanting to learn musical instruments every single day. There are times of year that are potential jackpots for tutors, and If you haven't been appropriately prepared before, the new year is always a great time for new students. So many people receive instruments as gifts, and many more commit to resolutions to learn to play 'this year', and you need to be there ready to take that call! The start of the school year is also often a rich period for tutors, with students starting new classes. You will be able to make several hundred pounds a month just by letting your immediate circle know you're giving lessons. More still when your website and social media are backing you up.

We should deal with the prospect of failure, because it has to be a possibility. I consider it less likely that you will fail yourself than somebody else will fail you, and as a result I would always advocate working for yourself over working for someone else. What better motivation could you possibly have for doing everything you can to be a success than enjoying one hundred percent of the rewards? If you work hard at it and make a load of money, you'll have nobody to thank but yourself. If you sit and watch TV all day pretending that you're 'working on your music' like some of the kids I used to know years ago, well… they're the guys working in the supermarket, wishing they'd done things differently.

This is not empty flattery, it is a simple fact: if you work hard, you will succeed. If you are willing to accept opportunity when it presents itself: you will succeed. If you resist the temptation to bleach your hair, lose a hundred pounds in body weight and head for the TV talent show audition circuit: you will succeed. But only you can decide what success means to you. This book speaks of making £30,000 a year with music and that being an income sufficient to sustain you, and I think that is a good place to start. By all means, aspire to more, but the goal is to have enough and to enjoy your work. When it comes to music as a passion, we should probably agree it is 'work' rather than really work. It may occasionally be a total drag, but I bet you never wish you were back at your old job. I know I never do.

DO NOT LET ANYBODY ELSE DEFINE YOUR SUCCESS. I have had people over the years imply (or tell me straight!) that I am a failure because I am not a chart-topping artist. That I can't be a 'real' musician if the person levelling it at me hasn't heard of me or seen me on TV. Just as we define our own success, we define our failure. If I really have failed yet I am left with a house, a car, no need to worry about bills and a life where through living within my means I am very happy, I'll go see if I can feel sad about that. That doesn't feel like a failure to me. Failure to me would be spending my life doing something I hate, feeling trapped by the trappings of a life I don't even want. Not being able to free myself from a career because I wouldn't be able to sustain the lifestyle I have grown to expect with anything less than the purgatory I am subjecting myself to. Ultimately, that failure manifests itself only with hindsight when those days are done, and the only question is how long will you wait to do something about it?

If something doesn't go your way, learn from it. Be determined to do take the experience for what it is and move forward, knowing that you're already one step closer to getting it right next time; because you've learned what not to do. It is not a failure unless you give up, and with so many opportunities out there you'd have to be crazy to do that.

Opportunities have come to me post-music that mean I work outside of it as well, and no part of me considers that a failure. I use my unique set of skills in literature (from school), in technology (from the day job) and in music (from a lifetime of playing) to carve a niche in the world where there isn't as much competition. Most recently I've branched into the development of software tailored specifically toward musicians. By thinking like a musician, I hope I can create tools that will be intuitive to musicians, helping them to create more music, and with luck helping me to remain solvent. Five years ago, I would not have seen that as a possibility, but doors opened as a direct consequence of my musicianship. And they will open for you too.

If you're competent with an instrument, and if you have been playing for a couple of years, or are willing to put in plenty of work perfecting your recorded work you are competent enough. You can be a successful musician. You will make money in music. You will make a very healthy second income while you're on your way to success, as well as providing yourself with a safety net for rainier days. Once you are in a position to work for yourself and commit your time to the advancement of your career, you will find you want to go to work, and that you're often still working into the night. That never used to happen to me at the day job.

Once you are making money in music, make sure to help other musicians understand the possibilities out there. The more accomplished and established you become, the more opportunities will come to you. And one day you will be able to pay it forward like my old guitar teacher, by referring work to the next group of musicians working their way up.

The strategies laid out in this book are those that worked for me, but there will be hundreds more. There will be several that resonate with you based on your own personal composition of skills and experience. Explore them, and do not be afraid to pursue them if that inner voice tells you they're worth the time and effort. Make sure you listen to that inner voice. Even if you don't trust it at first, make sure you hear it. Your confidence will build with each success.

You might catch that elusive lucky break and end up becoming a star, and if you do I'd be very grateful if you could swing by and buy me a beer. Whether you win the superstar lottery or not, you can make money in music, and there is no better time to start than the present.

My thanks for reading this book, I hope it proves inspirational, and that your career as a musician is everything you hope for.

Paul 'Ren' Reynolds